Susan Margaret McKinnon St. Maur Somerset

Impressions of a Tenderfoot During a Journey in Search of Sport in the Far West

Susan Margaret McKinnon St. Maur Somerset

Impressions of a Tenderfoot During a Journey in Search of Sport in the Far West

ISBN/EAN: 9783744795937

Printed in Europe, USA, Canada, Australia, Japan

Cover: Foto ©Andreas Hilbeck / pixelio.de

More available books at **www.hansebooks.com**

IMPRESSIONS OF
A TENDERFOOT

*DURING A JOURNEY IN SEARCH OF SPORT IN
THE FAR WEST.*

BY

MRS. ALGERNON ST. MAUR.

"Ye who love the haunts of Nature,
Love the sunshine of the meadow,
Love the shadow of the forest,
Love the wind among the branches;
And the rain shower and the snow storm,
And the rushing of great rivers
Through their palisades of pine-trees,
And the thunder in the mountains! Stay and listen.
  *   *   *   *
From the forests and the prairies,
From the great lakes of the northland."
                              Longfellow.

WITH MAP AND ILLUSTRATIONS.

LONDON:
JOHN MURRAY, ALBEMARLE STREET.
1890.

TO

MY DEAR SISTERS,

WHO ASKED FOR AN

ACCOUNT OF OUR WANDERINGS IN THE NORTH WEST,

THIS LITTLE BOOK IS AFFECTIONATELY

Dedicated.

THE HOUSE AT FINDLAY CREEK.

INTRODUCTION.

AFTER many months spent in wandering, when the excitement of changing scenes and varied incidents has ended, the traveller naturally wishes to collect the impressions made, and to put them in a tangible form, especially if, as in my case, he has never before been beyond the beaten track.

Ruskin has said that a human soul can do nothing better than "see something, and tell what it saw in a plain way." This I have tried to do, but, from lack of literary skill, the following pages may not suggest to the reader all the wonder and pleasure I experienced among the strange and often beautiful scenes they describe. I would fain have given more glowing descriptions than those I find in my note-books, of the wondrous cities I saw, full of energetic, industrious people, with many of whom we spent most delightful days; of noble rivers and far-reaching railroads, by which long distances were traversed with ease, and where grand mountains and valleys were all too quickly passed; of great primeval forests which the axe has not yet despoiled; and of quaint, peaceful Indian villages, where sunsets seemed to linger, illuming and transfiguring all the bare and primitive surroundings with soft, deep shadows and a poetry quite their own. How true it is that "one goes from Dan to Beersheba and says it is all barren, and another has seen heaven and angels in the way." To me the mental exhilaration of fresh scenes and fresh faces was a continual delight, and in recalling those scenes and faces I have been prompted to put memories and notes together, and, with the addition of my few hastily-drawn sketches, I now venture to offer the result to any one who, in lenient mood, will care to accompany me over the many leagues of our travels in this, my first essay in literature.

I have chosen the title "Impressions of a Tenderfoot" in order that those who read may not expect great things, a "Tenderfoot" meaning in the "Far-West," a person new to the country, or, must it be confessed, a "Greenhorn." Thus regarded, I trust that the contents of this volume may meet with a generous and lenient handling.

We undertook our journey in search of health, sport, and pleasure. We found these in different degrees, but the total far exceeded our expectations, and although our visible trophies are less numerous than they might have been under other conditions, the experiences we had together are a fund of delightful reminiscence for the years to come, when the now willing feet will have to be content to travel nearer and smoother paths.

S. St. M.

CONTENTS.

CHAPTER I.
THE VOYAGE—LAND—QUEBEC.

Liverpool—The *Parisian*—Discomforts of travel—St. Pierre—A faithless emigrant—Rimouski—Quebec—Falls of Montmorency—Montreal—Toronto—A "slaughter sale"   PAGE 1

CHAPTER II.
FROM TORONTO TO NORTH BAY BY THE GREAT LAKES.

Niagara—Canadian loyalty—The Canadian army—Untutored courtesy—The Canadian Pacific Railway: their cars and officials 13

CHAPTER III.
JOURNEY TO WINNIPEG—THE PRAIRIE TO CALGARY.

Railway discomforts—Chapleau—Railway fare—Lake Superior—Fellow-travellers—Dangers of the ice—Fort William—Winnipeg—Lord Wolseley's Red River expedition—The prairie—Regina—Blackfoot and Cree Indians—Buffalo—Calgary 23

CHAPTER IV.
CALGARY—MITFORD.

Life on a ranche—A private railway accident—Cochrane—Gophers—A horse ranche—"The jumping pound"—Customs of the Indians—A rough life—Native flowers—A coal-mine—I take charge of the live stock—A cow boy's outfit—The timber limits—Another railway accident.. 35

CONTENTS.

CHAPTER V.
BANFF—GOOD FISHING IN MINNEWONKA LAKE.

Banff—Up the Bow River—Minnewonka Lake—The Stony Indians—A 28lb. trout—The National Park—*Ovis Montana*—A good basket of fish—A rough Yorkshireman—Records of the Hudson's Bay Co.—Legend of Lake Minnewonka—Hot springs 52

CHAPTER VI.
VANCOUVER—VICTORIA.

To Vancouver—Vermilion Lakes—Scaling the Rocky Mountains—Golden City—Engineering feats—Glacier house—A missionary in difficulties—Comforts for sick travellers—Chinese labourers—The Fraser River—Yale—Vancouver—Vancouver Island—Victoria—Mr. Dunsmuir—The Indians—Expedition to Cowichan Lake—A tame bear—Forest trees—Tree grouse, or fool hens—My first camping experience—" Cowichan Hotel " 66

CHAPTER VII.
COWICHAN LAKE—OUR HAWATI INDIANS—DOWN THE RAPIDS.

Our Hawati Indians—Roughing it—Trout fishing—A healthy life—Indians and alcohol—Shooting the rapids—The charms of open air life—Guamachen Hotel 84

CHAPTER VIII.
VICTORIA—PORTLAND—NOTES ABOUT ALASKA.

Victoria—Indian rising on the Skena River—The Chinese quarter—Anecdote of the Princess Louise—Voyage to San Francisco—Tacoma—Precocious children—Columbia River— Portland—A series of mishaps — Sacramento Valley — A skunk—Attractions of Alaska—Duncan's mission 97

CHAPTER IX.
SAN FRANCISCO AND CHINATOWN—THE CHINESE QUESTION.

San Francisco—Cable cars—Cliff House—The sea lions—Mr. Sutro's gardens—Matthew Arnold's Civilization in

CONTENTS.

America—American popular literature—Chinatown—Joss
houses—Chinese customs—American dislike of the Chinese
—Baron v. Hubner's opinion—The Chinese question .. 108

CHAPTER X.
SAN FRANCISCO—MONTEREY—JOURNEY TO VANCOUVER.

San Francisco — Cliff House —Sea bathing—Woodward's
Gardens—Mission schools for Chinese children—Occidental Hotel—*Pamelos*—Cliff House—Monterey—Sea
bathing—The Monterey pine—Accident to a horse—
Journey to Portland—Discomforts of railway travelling
—Puget Sound 123

CHAPTER XI.
VANCOUVER—CANOEING IN HOWE SOUND.

Vancouver again—Large trees—The timber of British Columbia—Clearing building lots—The Indian village—
Reckless workmen—Important law-suit—Excursion to
the "North Arm"—Expedition to Howe Sound—Camping out—Native bear story—Sunday in camp—"A
smudge"—Squawmish Place—Mosquitoes—A long paddle 133

CHAPTER XII.
GLACIER HOUSE—THE COLUMBIA RIVER.

Start for Glacier House—Jackass Mountain—The Cariboo
mines—*Auri sacra fames*—Surveying the Selkirk Mountains—The glaciers—Rev. W. S. Green—Finding Columbus' anchor—Navvies as art patrons—Journey to
Golden City—On the Columbia River—The Kootenay
Indians—Habits of the miners—A Western man—Vicissitudes of life—At Windermere— A race for a claim .. 146

CHAPTER XIII.
SAM'S LANDING—THE TRAIL TO FINDLAY CREEK—THE PONIES.

Sam's landing—Native ponies—Geological terraces—Bunch
grass—Findlay Creek—Fishing—Vitality of bear—Kettle
River—" Panning out " gold—Deserted log-houses—Extravagance of miners—Trip to Canal Flat—Startled mule
teams—Life at Findlay Creek—A horse thief 162

CONTENTS.

CHAPTER XIV.
FISHING—MINERS—ALGERNON'S DIARY.

Start for a hunting expedition—Amateur doctoring—An afternoon sport—Miners' opinion of English ladies—A reticent Indian—Miners as literary critics—A day's washing—White squaws—The camp at Skookum-Chuck—A stampede—A grey wolf 176

CHAPTER XV.
IN SEARCH OF BETTER SPORT—LIFE AT FINDLAY CREEK—GOOD-BYE—DAYS ON THE TRAIL.

In search of better sport—Difficulties of mining—Capla—Prairie Indians—An Austrian hunting party—The stage waggon—Intense cold—Good-bye to Findlay Creek—The force of habit 189

CHAPTER XVI.
BREWER'S "STOPPING-HOUSE"—HOT SPRINGS—INDIAN WOMEN—FROM WINDERMERE TO GOLDEN CITY.

Mrs. Brewer on manners—Gold nuggets—Hot Springs—Indian squaws—Sick travellers—The Windermere Hotel—"Bull's Ball"—The "Marion"—Wild fowl—Shushwaps—Wheelhouse as my bedroom—Dutch Pete—American whist 200

CHAPTER XVII.
NOTES ABOUT EARLY FRENCH SETTLERS—HUNTING IN THE MOUNTAINS.

Banff Springs Hotel—Early French settlers—Extracts from letters—Trade as the only field of action—Prohibition of spirituous liquors—Algernon's diary—Horse Thief Creek—A bad shot—A narrow escape—Heavy snowstorm—The tracks of a grizzly—Whisky Hill—A deep cañon—Tepés of Shushwaps—A rough trail—A Yankee editor—A rat hunt 214

CHAPTER XVIII.
THE PRAIRIE—WINNIPEG—MOOSE-HUNTING—MANITOBA.

The prairie—Winnipeg—Indian characteristics—A great English horse—The prairie in winter—House of Legislature—Monsieur Narquet—Indian curios—Old Fort Garry—Hudson's Bay stores—The last buffalo—Moose-hunting—More about moose 236

CHAPTER XIX.

LIFE IN A LUMBER-CAMP.

Life in a lumber-camp—Interior of our tent—Food—Camp birds—Sauteaux Indians—Whitehead the engineer—A little brown squirrel—The foreman's chest—A bear story—Stream-driving—15° below zero—Buccaro Jimmy—Sunday in camp—Our tent on fire—Brot Harte's descriptions—The foreman's letter   247

CHAPTER XX.

HOMEWARD BOUND.

Homeward bound—A dreary landscape—Library at Ottawa—Chaudière Falls—A visit to the Museum—Yukon River—American hospitality—Tiffany's—Pea-nuts—Home again   269

LIST OF ILLUSTRATIONS.

OUR HUNTING COSTUME	*Frontispiece*	
A BLACKFOOT INDIAN	*To face page*	32
INDIAN TEPÉS ON THE PRAIRIE	,, ,,	48
THE BOW RIVER	,, ,,	64
THE COLUMBIA RIVER	,, ,,	154
WINDERMERE, BRITISH COLUMBIA	,, ,,	160
FINDLAY CREEK	,, ,,	178
MAP	*At end*	

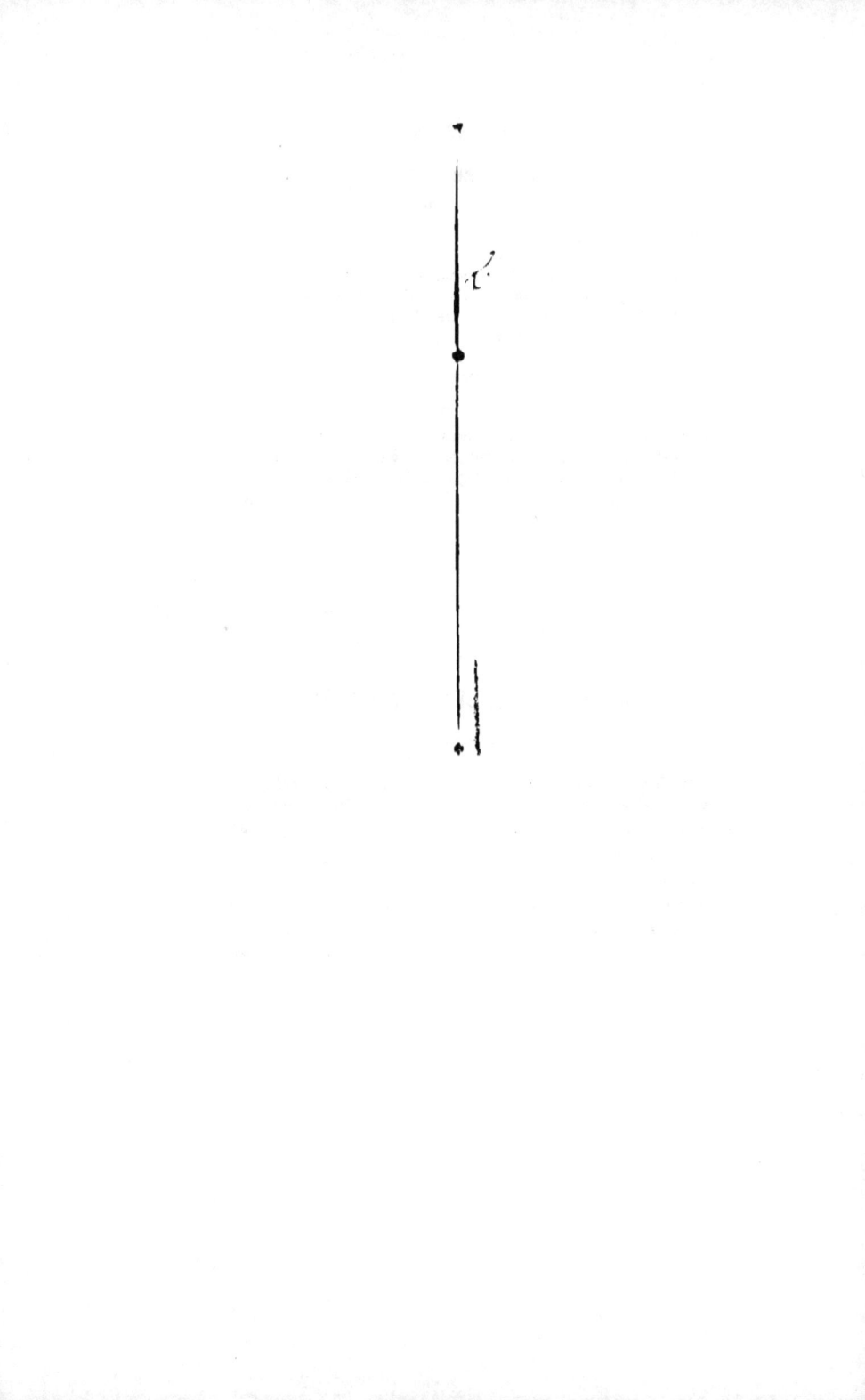

IMPRESSIONS OF A TENDERFOOT.

CHAPTER I.

THE VOYAGE—LAND—QUEBEC.

"For we are all, like swimmers in the sea,
Poised on the top of a huge wave of fate
Which hangs uncertain to which side to fall;
And whether it will heave us up to land,
Or whether it will roll us out to sea,
Back out to sea, to the deep waves of death,
We know not, and no search will make us know,
Only the event will teach us in that hour."
Matthew Arnold.

May 2nd.—What a glorious evening it was, our last for some time in dear old England. What brilliant effects of sun and cloud! the first pale shades of green in the budding trees harmonizing well with the russet browns of the bare pastures and wooded hollows.

It was nearly dark when we reached Liverpool; the great river, flowing silently between huge buildings with their tall chimneys, seemed ghostlike and weird, while innumerable glimmering lights from both houses and ships helped to add a mysterious attraction to the scene through the grey mists of an early summer night.

What endless thoughts were mine!—of kind friends left behind, of pleasant memories; what hopes for the future, and through all, what anticipations of seeing great and unknown lands beyond the wide seas!

To Algernon these pleasures were not new, for he had trodden many of these "happy hunting-grounds" before; still, he was keen to go again, and no one understands nor appreciates more than he the freedom of life in the Far West.

May 3rd.—We left Liverpool at 4 o'clock on a steam tug from the docks, to join the Allan Line's best steamer, the *Parisian*. Half an hour on a very rough sea was most trying; the passengers were crowded together like sheep in a pen, with all the baggage huddled round anyhow, the sea sweeping the deck of the tug every few minutes in a way which made it difficult to keep dry; thus we reached the steamer, and found some of the passengers, who had been wiser than ourselves, comfortably settled, having embarked before she left the dock. We reached Loch Foyle at 8 the following morning, and there had to await the arrival of the mails.

The *Parisian* is a fine steamer of 5300 tons, and Captain Smith, her commander, is a favourite with every one.

We had already many emigrants on board. Here more joined, making their number over 800; cabin passengers, intermediate and crew made another 200.

May 5*th.*—After leaving Loch Foyle, we had rough weather, and my experiences resulted in no literary suggestions.

All voyages are alike in so far that they have a beginning and an end; therefore, being a bad sailor myself, I intend to say as little about this part of my travels as possible. To see the world, one must become callous to personal comfort; travelling does all men good; they find their level, come in contact with the enterprise of others, and see life from many different points of view; and the results of wandering to and fro upon the earth are often garnered stores of wisdom.

How true are Laurence Oliphant's ideas on this subject!
" The proverb that a rolling stone gathers no moss is, like
" most proverbs, neater as an epigram than as a truth, in so
" far as its application to human existence is concerned.
" Even if by 'moss' is signified hard cash, commercial and
" industrial enterprises have undergone such a change since
" the introduction of steam and electricity, that the men
" who have made most money in these days are often those
" who have been flying about from one quarter of the world
" to another in its successful pursuit—taking contracts,
" obtaining concessions, forming companies, or engaging in
" speculations, the profitable nature of which has been
" revealed to them in the course of their travels. But
" there may be said to be other kinds of moss besides
" money, of which the human rolling stone gathers more
" than the stationary one. He meets with adventures, he
" acquires new views, he undergoes experiences, and gains

"a general knowledge of the world, the whole crystallising
"in after life into a rich fund of reminiscences, which
"becomes the moss that he has gathered."

Thursday, 10*th.*—A glorious day. A school of whales, some icebergs, and several Newfoundland fishing schooners have been sighted. Owing to the Straits of Belleisle being full of ice, our captain has been obliged to enter the Gulf of St. Lawrence by Cape Breton, which will take two days longer.

Two years ago the Atlantic steamers to Quebec were delayed seven days at the Straits of Belleisle, wedged in by ice floes on every side. The cold and discomfort experienced by the passengers were very great, as the provisions did not hold out.

The *Sardinian* that same year was nineteen days making Quebec, the ship getting among icebergs and thick fog.

The first land seen this morning, the Island of St. Pierre, belongs to France, and has a French marquis as Governor. It is an important place so far as the fishing industries are concerned, and all sailors in the French navy are obliged to serve a sort of apprenticeship with the fishing-boats in these seas before joining the regular navy. At the present time, the French are giving us some trouble, claiming fifteen miles of coast as their right on the shores of Newfoundland in connection with these fisheries.

Great excitement on deck at a supposed line of icebergs,

the owners of telescopes and field-glasses vying with each other in their eagerness to discover what they might or might not be. After some suspense and on nearer inspection the supposed line of icebergs proved to be the coast of Newfoundland, the high cliffs of which were white with snow. Before evening land was viewed on both sides of the ship, Cape Ray on the right, Cape Breton on the left.

As one gazes on the horizon out at sea, it seems strange to a novice that with such a boundless extent one can really see little more than from six to eight miles. When a ship is coming into view, the upper spars are visible at a much greater distance, being naturally above the limited horizon of the sea; for the same reason, land can often be seen at a great distance, and if the country be mountainous as far as forty or fifty miles.

Some years ago, Captain Smith was asked to take charge of a young woman who was going out to be married in Canada. The lover had sent £120 for her outfit and expenses. Before half the voyage was over the young woman came to the Captain, and told him she had changed her mind, having met a "new" man on the steamer whom she liked better, and him she intended to marry. Protests were useless; she married her fellow-passenger the day the ship arrived at Quebec. The rejected suitor had only an interview with the Captain to console him for the loss of his money and his bride.

May 12*th*.—Glorious sunshine, which made one forget

the trials of the early part of the voyage. At 8 A.M. we passed the Island of Gaspé, and after that saw the Canadian coast more clearly; black, bare, and rugged it all looked, some scattered fir and pine trees standing out plainly against the cold-looking rocks, the deep gullies of which, still full of snow-drifts, made the scene appear most wintry. As we steamed along, small fishing-villages came in view, with cultivated patches of land here and there. The emigrants could not conceal their disappointment with their first glimpse of Canada; but with its marvellous resources, doubtless in a few years their ideas will change. First impressions are not always to be trusted.

On arriving at Rimouski the pilot and health officers came on board; here we were delayed for nearly an hour, one of the emigrants refusing to be vaccinated. However, on being threatened with quarantine for six weeks, his scruples were overcome, and he submitted to the operation. The Canadian laws are very strict regarding vaccination, as a few years ago they had a terrible epidemic of small pox in Montreal and Quebec.

At this place disembarked two very rough-looking lumbermen, brothers, who were among our cabin passengers, returning from Belfast, where they had been to receive money left to them. They had inherited £80,000; neither of them could write his name. One was a hunchback, who had worked for twenty-eight years as cook in a lumber camp. So does the wheel of Fortune turn!

Sunday, May 13th.—

"'Tis always morning somewhere, and above
The awakening continents from shore to shore
Somewhere the birds are singing evermore."

Pleasant morning thoughts are these of the American poet and singer.

On deck at 6.30 to see the far-famed view of Quebec from the St. Lawrence. Alas! the morning was wet and misty; we passed the Falls of Montmorency, and ended our voyage at Point Levis, crossing to Quebec in the ferry boat; but even from that shrouded glimpse of the Heights of Abraham we realized how few were the scenes that could rival the incomparable beauty of that ancient fortress and quaint old city towering high above the noble river, of which all Canadians are so justly proud.

May 14th.—Quebec is an old-fashioned place, with a French-looking and, for the most part, a French-speaking population. Even the houses in the lower quarter of the town have a foreign look about them, with their green outside shutters and their tin roofs, while over the shop doors still hang quaint old French signs. The carriages chiefly used are French calèches, the models of which doubtless came from France during the reign of Louis XIV., when the impoverished gentilhomme became the unwilling emigrant; odd-looking vehicles they are, these high two-wheeled carriages on their loose springs, carrying two persons inside, and the driver perched on his little seat just above his horse, but admirable and easy for going over very rough roads; outside the town these were very rough, owing to the lateness of the spring, the frost not being yet out of the ground, and great banks of snow still lying on either side.

Quebec has never gone ahead like other cities in the Dominion, and is now rather taking a retrograde movement, the result of the decline in her timber trade, which never recovered the effects of a strike some years ago, when, owing to a rise in wages, most of the lumber business went to Montreal and Three Rivers. Large fortunes were made in Quebec in the lumber trade at one time; those days are past, and the inhabitants are no longer the wealthy citizens they were.

We visited the Falls of Montmorency. An introduction to Mrs. P. proved useful; she was most kind, and we followed her down a long flight of rather slippery wooden steps to a summer-house half-way below the falls, where we saw a wild rush of snow water surging with irresistible force over the high rocks, it being here the river takes its last mad plunge into the St. Lawrence.

The old gateways of the town no longer exist, having been demolished by some Vandal mayor of Quebec, who built "nice new ones" in their places, thereby, alas! destroying much of the historical interest of the city.

We spent two hours at the citadel, walking round the fortifications. A magnificent landscape extended far beneath us: the great St. Lawrence wending its way majestically to the sea; the country dotted over with villages and churches all along the river's course; opposite to Quebec the rising town of Point Levis; further down on the same side as Quebec, Beauport, and further still the spray rising from the Falls of Montmorency; and as the river receded further into the sunshine and the mist, losing itself at length in the far distance, this glorious panorama suggested one of Turner's grandest effects of sunshine and cloud.

We left Quebec this afternoon, making our first journey in a Pullman car. In the districts round the town, we passed through large tracts of country cut up into small farms; the people have lived on them thus from generation to generation, bettering their condition but little, selling their hay crops, and growing all else they require on their own bits of land. Further west much is achieved by toil and thrift, but these old settlers seem to have little idea of progression.

May 16th, Hotel Windsor, Montreal.—A fine hotel, fitted with every possible convenience. We paid $6 per day each person; this included everything except wine. We had an excellent suite of rooms, with a bath-room attached, and could order what we liked in the dining-room provided it was mentioned on the long "menu" for the day. Everything was detailed on this "menu," beginning with breads and rolls of all kinds.

Our introductions were not of much use to us here, as we found that Sir G. Stephen and Sir Donald Smith were both away at the Sault Ste. Marie.

We drove round the mountain, and from there had

magnificent views of the river, town, and surrounding landscape. Our way home took us through the beautiful cemetery, the trees all bursting into leaf, fitting emblems of the hope for those lying there so silently. A fine monument, presented by the citizens of Montreal, marks the remains of all firemen killed on duty in this city; the dangers of their calling are much greater here than in England, owing to the large number of wooden houses.

This place is much changed since Algernon was here in 1870. The Canadian Pacific Railway station stands where he remembers the old Main Guard to have been; he also pointed out a small hospital in Notre Dame Street which was the mess-house of the 60th Rifles. The town has enormously extended since that time, there being a great number of excellent shops: a dollar seems to go little further than a shilling does at home. Bought some blankets for camping and travelling in out of the way places. It is always desirable to have one's own, as at any of the small stopping-houses and hotels there is risk in using those provided: mountain fever can be carried in this way.

Queen's Hotel, Toronto, May 19*th.*—This town is the seat of a University, has a cathedral, many fine churches, and other large public buildings.

The hotel is an old-fashioned place, the cooking rather messy; the work is done by negro servants; those who waited at table showed us to our places with the greatest deference, but once there they did not mind how long they kept us waiting for our dinner, and when they did bring it, dashed the dishes down in front of us as if they were conferring a favour, and dealing a pack of cards; they slipped about with their great flat feet, reminding us of ducks by their movements. Negroes detest being called niggers; they prefer being designated coloured men— coloured gentlemen still better.

Buckwheat cakes and maple syrup I tasted here for the first time; both were excellent.

Wine was very expensive at all these hotels; no light claret procurable under $1 a bottle; champagnes were as much as $14 a bottle. Most people drank tea, coffee, or iced water during lunch or dinner. We were here offered butter-milk; this I declined. At the " Bars " of the hotels cocktails and all kinds of drinks can be procured at from 10 to 25 cents each.

May 21*st.*—Dined at Government House with Sir Alexander Campbell and his charming little daughter Miss Marjorie; we saw many pretty women while in Canada, but she was quite the prettiest. Afterwards went to a " Fancy Fair," in aid of an Art Institute which the people are anxious to build, so as to have a suitable place for their annual exhibition of pictures by Canadian artists. In this scheme both Lord Lansdowne, who was the late Governor-General, and Lady Lansdowne took much interest. Algernon met here many old friends, who gave us a kind welcome to Toronto.

I was told that although clothing and all imported goods

were expensive, the prices of bread, meat, and other provisions were extremely reasonable. House-rent, however, was high, and I was somewhat amused to hear that certain acquaintances Algernon asked after had gone to Europe for economy. People who were furnishing a house here, told us that they had many difficulties to contend with; that only very plain furniture of a regulation pattern was to be procured in Canada, and that before duty and carriage were paid on anything they obtained from England or New York, nearly 60 per cent. on the cost of the whole was charged.

A "Slaughter Sale" of dry goods or a "Slaughter Sale of Babies' Buggies" were startling announcements over shop windows; these were, I found, the terms used for clearing sales, dry goods, meaning silks, muslins, &c.; babies' buggies, an Americanism for children's perambulators. No doubt often one word is as good as another, but the unusual always attracts attention.

CHAPTER II.

FROM TORONTO TO NORTH BAY BY THE GREAT LAKES.

"Ye who love
The shaggy forests, fierce delights
Of sounding waterfalls, of heights
That hang like broken moons above,
With brows of pine that brush the sun,
Believe and follow."

Toronto, May 23*rd.*—A glorious day for visiting Niagara. We left the hotel soon after 7 A.M., and took our places in a first-class railway car. Into this tumbled all sorts and conditions of men, and it was not long before I realized the fact that the first class in this country is on a par with the third at home, there being no second or third class carriages used; and unless places can be taken in a sleeping or drawing-room car, one is sometimes obliged to travel with the roughest people.

We passed through a good farming country. All along the shores of Lake Ontario the land is in an excellent state of cultivation, but many burnt stumps are seen among the growing crops. How to get rid of these hindrances to husbandry is a difficult problem. Labour is so valuable that time cannot be spared to dig them out at once, so a few are removed year by year by burning and grubbing.

It would be impossible for me to describe the unspeakable vastness and grandeur of Niagara, but as our visit there was part of our pleasant Canadian travels, I cannot pass it by without briefly giving my impressions.

As is well known, the Falls are best seen from the Canadian side. Goat Island divides the two falls. Clouds of spray and the noise of the great rushing waters were the first glimpse and sounds that met us. The American Fall is a vast volume of water, thundering down in a glittering cascade of white foam. But the Horse Shoe Fall! The memory of this will live through my lifetime. There we saw seas of bright green waters rolling over into the great gulf below. The majesty and immensity overwhelmed me. In presence of this mighty work of the great Creator, all—all seemed to sink into insignificance. The ills of life, the shortness of it, the disappointments and the joys—all were forgotten. We felt as if we had had a glimpse into the unseen, where strange forms moved in the great wreaths of mist and foam, and gleams of sunshine through the mysterious haze transfigured the face of the waters.

The surrounding woods were now full of song,—

> "And birds in blended gold and blue,
> Were thick and sweet as swarming bees;
> And sang as if in Paradise,
> And all their Paradise was spring."

When we first arrived in Canada they had not yet returned from the south. Now it interests me to watch them, as many of them are those I have not seen before: the golden oriole, waxwing, woodpeckers of different kinds, canaries and humming-birds—all of brighter hues than our familiar English birds. Even the thrush has here borrowed from the robin, and appears with a red breast.

Goat Island is on the American side. As we re-crossed the suspension bridge which unites Canada and America, men were busily employed in widening the bridge, and while I had to ask for the assistance of a hand, I saw men standing on the girders in perilous positions, driving great bolts home, apparently as much at their ease as if they had been on land, instead of appearing, as they did to me, suspended in mid air, with the rushing river below them.*

The hideous mills and glaring hotels, the tawdry shops, the noisy cab-drivers who implore to be hired, and lastly, the people who offer to be guides when you want none of them—all these things harshly jar upon my mind at a time when I would fain go silently on my way, and disappointed me in our visit to Niagara. There are many unnecessary ways of seeing the Falls to which the unsuspecting traveller becomes a victim, which add little to his pleasure. If willing to go, he is taken down damp and slippery steps, or "elevators," clothed in oilskins, to see the Falls from below, and hurried in a wild rush through spray which completely soaks him: confused in mind and

* This bridge has been carried away by a recent storm.

disturbed in body, he is thankful to emerge, thoroughly frightened, from what has appeared to him a most hazardous experience.

The best way, if one wishes to see the Falls from below, is to embark in *The Maid of the Mist*, a small steamer which runs up the river almost under the Horse Shoe Fall, looking from above like a cockle-shell bobbing up and down in the water.

Toronto, May 24*th.*—This is the Queen's birthday. The loyalty of the Canadians should make England blush. They are holding high holiday to-day because of it, and rejoicing most heartily, the whole town being *en fête;* and from almost every house a flag is flying, and the people, dressed in their holiday attire, are crowding down the principal streets.

All here seem to have the deepest affection for the mother country, and even those families who have been in Canada for several generations appear to have this feeling of love for the country of their forefathers in an extraordinary degree. Mr. Goldwin Smith, who has taken up his residence among these good people, may have a few followers, for he is an eloquent and able man, although his mind appears to have become warped and his sympathies alienated in a manner which many cannot understand. The handing over of Canada to the Americans, which he is perpetually advocating, can only meet with the universal condemnation it deserves among a loyal and upright people like the Canadians, who love their country and their Queen, and who hope to see the bonds that unite Canada to the mother country consolidated and strengthened as time goes on; whenever (in the words of General Lord Wolseley) "God in His mercy is pleased to send us a statesman wise enough and great enough to federate and consolidate into one united British empire all the many lands and provinces which acknowledge Queen Victoria as their sovereign."*

Most Canadians met in society have often been in England, and seem to know it better than their own country, for when they wish to travel they generally cross the Atlantic.

The Governor of Ontario, Sir Alexander Campbell, asked us to join his party for the races. The course lies on pretty undulating ground close to the shore of the lake. The meeting was held under the rules of the Ontario Jockey Club, and no betting was allowed. The Governor

---

* The late Right Hon. W. E. Forster, in an address to the Philosophical Institution of Edinburgh in 1875, says:—

"I believe that our union with our Colonies will not be severed, because I believe that we and they will more and more prize this union, and become convinced that it can only be preserved by looking forward to association on equal terms. In other words, I believe our colonial empire will last, because no longer striving to rule our Colonies as dependencies when they have become strong enough to be independent. We shall welcome them as our partners in a common and rising Empire." What more popular cry at present than the preservation of our colonial empire? Some twelve years ago, it is true, a voice from Oxford declared this empire to be an illusion for the future and a danger for the present; but Professor Goldwin Smith has gone to Canada, and his eloquent arguments for disruption have as little convinced the Canadians as ourselves.

and his party were treated with the greatest deference, and his carriages were the only ones allowed to drive up the course. Opposite the winning-post Sir Alexander Campbell had a charming box; in this we sat for most of the afternoon. There were some nice young horses, but the riding was very bad, so much so that one or two that ought to have been winners got into the second place. The crowd was quiet and orderly, two mounted police being sufficient to keep the course, and doing it extremely well; each of them was provided with a cutting whip, which they seemed to use pretty freely among the crowd. I thought of the questions which would be asked in the House, and of the rage of an English mob, if such a thing was even hinted at there.

Canada will soon possess a fine army of its own; the regulars are a splendid body of men, and besides these it has 40,000 Militia and Volunteers; in case of emergency all men over eighteen are liable to be called out for military service. This law was made at the time when the English troops were withdrawn.

The Police at Toronto equal the London Police in smartness and civility, and are dressed in exactly the same way. When Sir Alexander Campbell was Post-master-General he had the Postmen also dressed like those in England; until that time they had worn the same uniform as the American Postmen, which is ugly and unworkmanlike.

I have had several long and interesting conversations about the wheat-growing capacity of the country: here, as elsewhere, opinions differ much, but it is an undisputed fact that since 1882 there have only been two abundant harvests, that of last year being one of them. It is against the profitable working of the land that the season is so short and labour so expensive; and even if farmers get emigrants direct from the ships, they seldom remain with them long; the land fever is so strong, each wants to have a "holding" for himself, and this can still be obtained for a nominal sum.

Further west 160 acres can be bought for $10.

Colonel S——, with whom we dined last night, told us a curious story: When he came out to America, nearly twenty-five years ago, he was asked to take charge of a young lady on a journey from the States. Miss T—— was exceedingly beautiful. After they started, a Californian gold-digger got into the same car; he was a tall, rough-looking fellow, dressed in the usual Western fashion, with buckskin shirt, and trousers with fringes down the seams, long boots, and a broad-brimmed hat; he was armed with a revolver and a bowie knife, stuck into his belt. He sat down opposite Miss T——, and stared at her in a manner which greatly annoyed Colonel S——. Several times during the journey he was on the point of getting up and expostulating; as he expressed it: "It made my English blood boil to see the insolence of the fellow;" each time, however, Miss T—— prevented his doing so by whispering to him to sit still—that it did not in the least matter to her.

They got out at the next station; the man followed them:

on taking their seats again, the Californian, with the air of a prince, took off his hat, and feeling in his pocket, brought out a large nugget of gold, which he threw into the lap of the astonished girl, saying: "Heaven bless your pretty face; it's the prettiest face I've ever seen on God's earth. Keep that in remembrance of Jack ——," and was gone.

Colonel S—— told me he felt sure had he made the silghtest protest the man would have shot him dead; that it was only the calmness and coolness of Miss T—— that prevented this. He also added that, after twenty-five years' experience of the country and its people, he saw that what he had at the time mistaken for the most insulting conduct was in reality an act of untutored and involuntary homage to a beautiful woman.

May 25th.—Often in a journey plans and routes are changed, and a traveller may be unable to avail himself of introductions; but arriving as a stranger, if provided with letters to the right people it helps to make things much pleasanter, and he hears and sees many things which otherwise he would miss; and great trouble is generally taken in showing strangers all that is worth seeing. This we found frequently in our own case.

May 26th.—Said good-bye to Toronto and to my maid, as, after duly considering the matter, we found that it was impossible to take her with us. Travelling with a maid in this country is more trouble than can be imagined, as, except in the big towns, no accommodation is provided, and she is consequently always in the way; fortunately I was able to send mine to stay with her aunt at Chicago. She was regretful, but I felt I had acted wisely.

The lake route to Port Arthur is still closed on account of the ice in Thunder Bay. This chain of lakes is so immense that little land is seen during the voyage; and on Lake Huron especially tremendous storms frequently occur. For this and other reasons we had decided to join the Canadian Pacific Railway by a branch line from here, which takes us in one night's journey to a station called North Bay, the junction where we had to wait for the mail train from Montreal. After about an hour there we were glad at last to find ourselves really on our way to the Rocky Mountains.

The C.P.R. Co., as it is always called out here, have made their "Cars" as near perfection as is possible; nothing approaching their luxury and comfort is to be found on the American Continent—so many old travellers assured me. The sleeping cars which are used on long journeys have high-backed seats for two persons facing each other; at night these seats are arranged as beds, an upper berth being let down from above. There is a ladies' dressing-room at the end of the car but so many have to share this that it ceases to be a luxury. The most comfortable way when travelling is to engage the "State-room," which accommodates two persons; there being only one of these on each car, it is not always to be procured, sometimes being reserved several weeks before.

The railway officials are civil and obliging, and any

little service they may do is not from mercenary motives, as they always seem to think themselves quite one's equal. Rich Americans and others will, however, soon introduce the odious tipping system; the negro porter who has charge of the sleeper already looks out for his little present at the end of the journey: he does all he is asked on the cars, and is a great adept at making beds, when the time comes for all the passengers to turn in; but it makes it difficult to judge where to give and where not when the greatest offence is sometimes taken at the offer of money. These negro servants of the company are dressed in a serviceable grey serge uniform with brass buttons and cap to match; in the morning and evening when making the beds they wear white cotton jackets; they are always clean and tidy. I do not know much about negroes, but they look cleaner than white men would doing the same work, and they never appear fussed or overheated.

CHAPTER III.

JOURNEY TO WINNIPEG—THE PRAIRIE—TO CALGARY.

"'Tis with our judgments as our watches, none
Go just alike, yet each believes his own."

WE passed to-day through large tracts of cold and bleak-looking forest; here and there a mirror-like lake or mountain stream enlivened the scene. It is only after having been in the rugged vast wilderness of natural forest that we realise for the first time the enormous difficulties the settler has to overcome in making a farm-steading out of this chaos.

Settlers' shanties are to be seen from time to time as one goes along: at every station where we stopped groups of men were waiting to see the train pass; it was evidently the excitement of the day. The sight of new faces, the hope of seeing a friend pass by, or the chance of hearing a few words of news, are trivial events which have a wonderful power in a country where the requirements of the settler's life compel men to live apart from their fellows.

I really believe it is a kind dispensation of Providence

that they have to work so hard; and hence only a few realise and regret that there is little or no time for mental culture.

May 29*th*.—The constant noise in the train is very tiring, but as the pace is much slower than in England, it does not shake in the same way. Chapleau was the first place we saw this morning: we passed through a country of rocks and burnt woods, where forest fires seemed to have cleared out every living thing; but there is such a wealth of timber in the North-West that little is thought of fires, nor are the precautions to prevent them insisted on in the way they ought to be. When a forest fire begins it may go for miles, leaving nothing but complete desolation behind it. Everywhere one sees the ravages of past fires, whole tracts of forest with only the blackened and burnt stumps of trees remaining. As the country gets settled up no doubt these things will improve.

Near Messanabie, where Dog Lake is crossed, a short portage connects the waters flowing southwards into Lake Superior with those flowing northwards into Hudson's Bay. This is the old Dog Lake route by which many of the stores for the Hudson's Bay forts in the North-West went up, and by which the furs were sent down.

Dining cars are attached to the trains: these cars run 300-mile sections, returning the same distance the following day. The food provided is simple and good; supplies come chiefly from Winnipeg and Montreal, but the conductors have the power to buy fish, poultry, and whatever become necessary, at any of the stations that they pass. At one station, for instance, two Indians brought some wild ducks for sale, which our conductor bought.

Many people travelling do not care to enter the dining-car except for breakfast and dinner, as the latter is seldom later in the day than 6 o'clock.

The following is one day's menu, for which we were charged 75 cents, or about three shillings per meal:

BREAKFAST.

Fruits, Porridge and Cream, Tea, Coffee, Cocoa, Chocolate.
Fresh-boiled Trout, Beefsteaks with Mushrooms, English Bacon, Lamb Cutlets, Sweet-cured Hams, Eggs, Omelettes.

Breads.
Brown, Dipped Toast, Dry Toast, Graham Bread, Corn Bread, Hot Rolls.

LUNCH.

Cold meats, Stew, Californian Pears, Cheese and Biscuits, Tea and Coffee.

DINNER.

Kidney Soup, Salmon and Potatoes, Salmi of Duck, Roast Beef, Roast Lamb.
Rice Pudding, Cranberry Pies.
Cheese.
Dessert.

There were excellent clarets, spirits, and beer. The above, I think, proves that the comforts of the table are carefully studied by the Canadian Pacific Company.

At Mazokama, Lake Superior comes into view. The day

was not so clear as we would have wished, but the sharp and rugged edges of the cliffs, half hidden by mist, looked striking and impressive. There is still a great deal of ice all along the coast; the enormous extent of water makes it difficult to realise that this is a fresh-water lake. A chain of islands separate Nepigon Bay from the lake, and the shore of the bay is the line followed by the train to and from Nepigon station. Excellent trout fishing can be obtained in the Nepigon river, where 6-lb. trout are not uncommon.

On Lake Superior the large lake trout are numerous, white fish—*Coregonus albus*—also; these last are excellent eating; during the summer great numbers of them are caught, dried, and used in winter as one of the principal articles of food. The dogs which draw the traineaux are also fed with them, one dried fish being the daily allowance for each dog.

All sorts of people as our fellow-travellers. One little weasel-faced man, a German by birth, has been everywhere and seen everything, and is now travelling on some scientific expedition. He tells us he has spent the last two years among the Esquimaux, and shot many polar bears; he is now on his way to stay with two Indian tribes, in order to learn something of their language.

The Micmacs, in New Brunswick, are the only tribe who possess a written language. Some of the Indian legends are very pretty, but rarely can they be persuaded to tell them to strangers. Until after Winnipeg is reached most of the Indians are dressed in the same way as the white people, which costume does not at all suit the noble red man.

Port Arthur is beautifully situated on the west shore of Thunder Bay, now a flourishing town, and one of the great exporting places for grain. We had fine views of the famous Sleeping Giant mountain, behind which is the Silver Inlet, a mining locality which has yielded almost fabulous wealth.

The Canadian Pacific Company's steamers have been blocked in the ice for the last seven days, and were only extricated yesterday. One foolhardy passenger with several guides attempted, with the aid of a dog traineau, to reach the land, in order to avoid the vexatious delay; the ice, however, became so broken up before they had accomplished half the distance, that they were only rescued with considerable danger and difficulty by a relief party from the shore, who dragged a boat over the ice and through the water, arriving just in time, as these too adventurous people were completely exhausted.

All watches are put back one hour here, and another hour when we reach Winnipeg; they were put back four-and-a-half hours when crossing the Atlantic, and half an hour will also have to be deducted on reaching Calgary, so the difference of time between London and Calgary is seven hours. Thus, when it is but 5 P.M. here it is midnight in England.

Fort William, an old Hudson Bay post on the Kaministiquia river, affords extraordinary advantages for lake traffic. After this is passed, we reach a place called Savenne; there we saw two of the old boats built at Quebec and used by Lord Wolseley in 1870 on his way to Fort Garry, now Winnipeg.

At East Selkirk the line turns southward, and at St. Boniface the river is crossed by a long iron bridge, and Winnipeg is reached. It is now a flourishing town of 25,000 inhabitants, but at the time of Lord Wolseley's expedition it was only the principal Hudson's Bay trading-post, with little to be seen except the fort and a small settlement of about 250 to 300 people, chiefly known then as the centre of the half-breed rebellion under Louis Riel.

To reach Fort Garry, Lord Wolseley had to bring his troops by steamer to Thunder Bay, at the head of Lake Superior, and after making a road for forty miles through the woods to Lake Shebandowan, he accomplished the rest of the way by using the lakes, rivers and portages connecting them. I may add that the Kaministiquia and Matawan rivers were used to get both boats and stores to this point, as well as the road to Lake Shebandowan. It took his little force ninety-five days to complete a journey which we accomplished in forty-five hours.

It is very interesting to Algernon, seeing all this country again, as he was one of the officers with Lord Wolseley, who told me Algernon carried the heaviest pack during that expedition; and having both skill and experience in canoe work, he steered many of the boats down the most dangerous part of the rapids.

Winnipeg is situated on the isthmus of land formed by the junction of the Assiniboine and the Red rivers, is about

THE PRAIRIE.

ninety miles from the United States frontier, fifty miles south of the lake whose name it takes, and into which the Red river runs, opening up by water all the vast and fertile region of the Saskatchewan. The Saskatchewan river is 500 miles long, and drains an area of 25,000 square miles. As we intended to revisit Winnipeg, we only remained there a short time and then rejoined the "Cars."

From here to Brandon we pass through the great wheat country of Manitoba; after leaving Brandon we are really on the prairie—grass everywhere, and such grass !

Now and again the train stops, and we find ourselves in a prairie town, which appears to consist of an hotel (at the bar of which the most fiery whisky is to be had !) with several wooden houses scattered round it, and generally a few stray cattle.

Talking of hotels, when one enters the North-West Territory the prohibition of spirits is strenuously enforced, though, in spite of this, whisky seems to be generally procurable with a little management.

Portage la Prairie and Brandon are the two principal grain markets of the province.

In the Canadian North-West there are about 300 million acres of arable and pasture land, of which one-third or more may be capable of producing wheat of the finest quality.*

* "The Prairie Section (according to the Canadian Geological Survey Reports) may be said to extend from the Red river, on the 97th meridian W. from Greenwich, to Calgary, near the Rocky Mountains,

30   *IMPRESSIONS OF A TENDERFOOT.*   [CHAP.

Further on we passed Regina, the capital of Assiniboia; the Executive Council of the North-West Territory, em-

on the 114th meridian, a distance of 800 miles, and from the 49th to the 54th degrees of north latitude.

There are three distinct plateaux or steppes sloping from the Rocky Mountains, north-easterly towards Lake Winnipeg and the Red river, having well-defined escarpments running north-westerly parallel with the range.

The general slope from the foot-hills of the Rockies averages about five feet to the mile.

The lowest of these plateaux averages about 800 feet above the sea, and embraces an extensive lake system nearly 14,000 miles in extent, the largest, Lake Winnipeg, covering 8,500 square miles.

The total area, including the lakes, is 55,000 square miles.

This interior basin, the lowest of the continent, generally known as the Red River Valley, has perhaps the finest wheat-land in the world. It is only fifty-two miles wide at the International boundary, and rises thence southward for about 200 miles, attaining an elevation nearly one thousand feet above sea-level.

The second steppe is about 250 miles wide at the 49th parallel, and 200 miles at the 54th, having an area of over 100,000 square miles, 71,000 square miles of which form the eastern portion of the great plains. Its average elevation is 1,600 feet above sea-level.

The third steppe has an average elevation of 3,000 feet, being 4,000 feet at the foot-hills and 2,000 feet at its eastern edge. Its area is 134,000 square miles, of which 115,000 are almost entirely devoid of forest. Its breadth on the 49th parallel is 465 miles.

The total area south of the 54th parallel is 280,000 square miles—about 180,000,000 of acres; of which, after allowing for swamps and lakes, mountains and barrens, by far the greater portion is arable.

In a recent report of the Senate of Canada it is stated that this northern forest-covered region embraces also the greatest fur-producing country in the world, supplying three-fourths of all the valuable furs sold in Leipsic and London, to the annual value of millions of dollars.

The climate of the eastern slope of the Rockies for a belt of over 150 miles in width is, as compared with the plains on the same latitude eastward, exceptionally mild in winter. A south-west wind, bracing the provinces of Assiniboia, Alberta, Saskatchewan, and Athabaska, meet here. At this place also are the headquarters of the North-West Mounted Police, a military organisation numbering 1000, of whom Canada is justly proud, they being nearly all picked men, and under the strictest military discipline.

The country, though retaining all the characteristics of the prairie, is now more broken and undulating; deserted lakes and buffalo wallows become more frequent, and are favourite resorts of water-fowl of all kinds. Swans, cranes, geese, pelicans, and ducks of many varieties all frequent them; snipe, plover, curlew, and prairie chicken are also to be met with in this part of the country, while now and again the wandering coyoté may be seen skulking on his lonely way; antelopes are rare, being shy and timid animals, and therefore scared by the noise of

---

called the *Chinook*, blowing at right angles to and over the Rockies, brings a thaw, removing snow, and enabling cattle to feed out all the year round. At Canmore, in the Rockies, 4,200 feet above the tide, cattle range out during the winter. The remarkable warmth of a wind passing for hundreds of miles over snow-covered mountains, could not be accounted for by the proximity of the warm waters of the Pacific, but is explained by the alternate expansion and condensation of air flowing from the ocean level over the mountains, and descending thence to the plains below. As the moisture is evaporated or the air expanded in rising over the mountains, latent heat is absorbed, which is given out again by the condensation of the moisture or the compression of the air in descending to the plains below.

The Bow river coal area is estimated to contain 330,000,000 of tons, and will be the chief source of supply for the prairie region and for many hundred miles of railway, and an increasing source of traffic for the latter."—*President T. Keefer's Address to Am. Soc. C.E.*, 1888.

the passing trains. The prairie which we have traversed is all marked by the old trails of buffalo, and in some places their bones and skulls lie thickly scattered.

At Medicine Hat we saw many Blackfoot and Cree Indians, their reservations not being far off. Most of the squaws sat on the ground, huddled up in their coloured blankets, looking miserable enough, some of them smoking, and offering for sale polished buffalo horns, which are so scarce now that even those gathered off the prairie command a ready sale. The braves, in blankets of brilliant colours, stood talking in groups. One Indian papoose was looking longingly at an orange which a small white child was eating. I had just time, as the train moved off, to obtain three from the dining car and give them to the child; and the squaws bobbed their heads in acknowledgment, and giggled with pleasure as the papoose toddled towards them with the oranges in her small arms. Trifling incidents like this bring one into touch with the people, and gratify oneself as well.

A station garden was being made here, and seemed to be a novel and interesting sight to the inhabitants, who crowded round it. A man was busily engaged planting trees and flower-seeds, while at the other end of the garden two enterprising black pigs had entered unobserved through a hole in the fence, and were enjoying themselves vastly, ploughing up the soft earth with their snouts, until they were routed with ignominy by the aid of sticks and stones.

A BLACKFOOT INDIAN.

When Algernon was in Colorado in 1873, there were thousands of buffalo on the plains, and when he was coming eastwards the following year by the Kansas Pacific Railway, the train was stopped for many hours by the big herd crossing the line.

There were two herds, the "southern herd," which ranged between the River Platte and Old Mexico, and the "northern herd," which rarely crossed the Platte, and ranged as far north as the Great Slave Lake.

The last time the northern herd came north, over 800,000 were killed for their hides alone, which at that time were valued at $1 each. Now it is next to impossible to procure a good buffalo robe. A very fine one, which was sent to the Colonial Exhibition in London, was sold on its return to Toronto for $60—a great bargain.

No fence, however strong, stopped the buffalo. As the herd marched on, by sheer weight it broke down every impediment. If the leaders failed to do this, the animals behind pressed forward, walking over the bodies of those who fell in front.

With the march of civilization, they were bound in time to disappear, but the wanton destruction of these noble creatures seemed ruthless waste.*

We now saw glimpses of the Bow river; the undulations of the foot-hills were a relief after the level prairie

---

* Have just heard that the tame herd of buffalo near Winnipeg has been sold to a ranche in Texas for $18,000; only nine of these animals are pure bred, the remainder of the herd are crossed with Texan cows.

over which we had been travelling for two days, and we were glad to be nearing our journey's end.

In the old days before the railway, it was thought to be fast travelling to go from Winnipeg to the Rocky Mountains in six weeks. The same journey took us three days. We reached Calgary at two in the morning, having been much delayed by the heating of a wheel, which necessitated our frequently stopping to cool it down.

A lad killed a snake at one of the places where we stopped. There are a few rattlesnakes round Medicine Hat, but, with this exception, there are not many in this part of the country.

CHAPTER IV.

CALGARY AND MITFORD.

"What man would live coffined with brick and stone?
Imprisoned from the influences of air!
And cramped with selfish landmarks everywhere,
When all before him stretches furrowless and lone
The unmapped prairie none can fence or own."—*Lowell.*

Royal Hotel, Calgary, May 30th.—After a five days' journey, we were glad to leave the train; a dirty-looking room and not particularly clean-looking beds were not inviting; however, at 2 A.M. we had nothing to do but make the best of them. No baths were procurable this morning, and we had the toughest of beef-steaks for breakfast. This hotel seems used as a sort of club by many men coming in long distances from their ranches; when obliged to remain in town for the night they sit in the bar, talking and smoking in groups.

Calgary is the centre of the great ranching country, and one of the chief outfitting-places for the mining districts. We found it full of Cowboys and Indians; the shops which the latter seemed to appreciate were the butchers and photographers, some of their own portraits being for sale in the windows of the latter.

During dinner we had a message from the G——s to come and see them in their car. They were on their way to Toronto, and gave us charming accounts of the delights of their journey through the mountains.

A telegram from the C——s, telling us to come to Mitford this evening, was very welcome. The train to Vancouver does not pass till 2 A.M., so we were glad to go by a freight train passing in the afternoon.

It required some persuasion to induce the conductor of the freight train to take us with him; but ultimately he agreed to do so, and he helped us to get our baggage into the caboose.

When getting off at Mitford, Algernon offered him a couple of dollars for his trouble, but he shook his head and declined them with thanks. The gratuitous civility of some of the people here strikes one very pleasantly.

We received a most kind welcome from our friends, who have a nice little house.

Mitford, May 31st.—We have a beautiful view of the Rocky Mountains here, and on a fine morning it is difficult to believe they are sixty miles distant: we are surrounded by fine undulating prairie. The cattle are fat and sleek, though they have had nothing but what they could find on the "range" all winter. The great drawback here is the frost at night; even in summer there is often enough to injure the potatoes and wheat.

LIFE ON A RANCHE.

Adela and I amused ourselves planting the garden: we sowed cabbages, lettuces, cauliflowers, carrots, beet, and beans.*

The soil is surprisingly rich; one digs nearly a yard deep, and still it is the same good brown loam everywhere.

The saw-mill and house are close to the C.P.R.; at the former fifty men are at work. Their wages are from $20 to $30 a month, and they are boarded as well. A private railway brings the logs down from the forest, they are sawn up here and put in the cars for market.

N——, Tom C——, and Algernon have been busy this morning making a garden fence. They also are building a new hen-house; the latter requires to be well put together, to keep out the cold in winter, and has double walls, with saw-dust filled up between. Dug-out hen-houses with turf roofs also make warm shelter; only a few have stoves, and often the claws of the poor birds get frost-bitten. The cat here has had her ears frozen off; fortun... they both are gone just at the same place, and give her the appearance of having her ears cropped.

June 1st.—Mr. Kerfoot, a neighbour, and one of the best riders and drivers in the North-West, drove Adela's ponies in the buckboard. They have been on the prairie for six months; when "taken up" they often require re-breaking; one of them lay down twice, bucked, and made a great fuss. Mr. Kerfoot drove them patiently and well. The harness and buckboard, both of American make, were

* And heard afterwards everything had done well.

perfectly adapted to the rough roads and prairie work. These carriages, owing to the wide axle, are almost impossible to upset, and one can drive them where no English carriage could go. The harness enables the horses to go quite independently of each other; the pole-pieces, instead of being, as in England, fast to the head of the pole, are here attached to a short bar called the yoke, which works loosely on the end of it, and also gives the horses a straight pull in holding back.

We all started on the private railway to see the timber limits, which are fifteen miles distant. A truck was arranged for us to sit on in front of the engine, the latter pushing us along. The men in charge drove too fast, and when we had gone about three miles, we felt several great jolts, the truck had left the rails and upset; most fortunately for us, one of the wheels got wedged in the sand, and the brakesman, having put on the brakes, stopped the engine. For a few moments there was an awful feeling of suspense; we all expected the engine would come crashing down on the top of us; happily, however, this did not occur, else we might all have been killed. On regaining our feet, we found the only person badly injured was the brakesman; he, poor fellow, lay under the engine, with three bad wounds in his head, and his ear almost severed from the scalp. With difficulty he was extricated from his perilous position, and while the C———s and Algernon remained with him, N——— and I went for assistance.

We ran for three miles across the prairie, and sent for the

doctor—there was one fortunately only two miles off—and having procured a mattress, pillows, ether, and bandages, harnessed the buckboard; then there was a doubt if we could manage the ponies, which had been so refractory the day before. I undertook to drive, and kept them at full gallop the whole way. One condition I made before starting, that in going up the hill over very rough ground, as the ponies required my undivided attention, I was not to be allowed to be jolted out of the carriage.

The doctor came quickly, a waggon followed, the poor fellow was soon in his little bed at the saw-mills, and, wonderful to relate, though so terribly injured, and with a badly-fractured skull, he recovered. It is always much in favour of these men during illness that they have lived a hardy out-of-door life.

June 2nd.—Drove to the British American Co.'s sheep-ranche. The manager was away, but his housekeeper gave us luncheon; afterwards we went out fishing. We caught nineteen trout; having heard how easy it was to catch fish here, we were disappointed at finding them very shy. A thunder-storm was going on most of the time, which may have been the reason of our want of success. Here the fish take best on a bright sunny day—just the contrary to what they do in England.

We went on later to the store at Cochrane, kept by a Frenchman, who had previously lived all his life in Paris. He said he was doing pretty well, but the prairie life seemed somewhat to depress him.

June 3*rd.*—The doctor who comes to see the man who was hurt in the engine, has travelled much, and was for a long time in the Hudson Bay Co.'s service. He told me that when at Moose Factory he had an excellent team of ten Esquimaux dogs, and had on one occasion driven them to Albany, a distance of 110 miles, in 24 hours, returning the same distance two days later. The old breed of Esquimaux dogs is very scarce now; we saw a team in Calgary, the leaders being the only fine ones; for this pair the owner was offered £100, which he refused.

June 4*th.*—10° of frost last night.

Algernon went for a ride with Mr. Kerfoot, and in the afternoon we all rode over to his horse-ranche. The horses are most clever in avoiding the gopher holes, and if given their heads they can go at any pace over them without making a mistake.

Gophers abound here; in places the prairie is full of their burrows, and being a kind of marmot, they live underground.

At the ranche we saw more than a hundred horses. The corrals are wonderfully well arranged, three opening into each other. When the band of horses has been driven into the first, which is the largest, the horses required for branding or breaking are separated from the rest, and, the gate being opened, are turned into the second corral. The entrance into the third corral is by a very high and strong gate, so arranged as to swing round against the side of this corral, with just space for a horse to stand between.

A single horse is now let through this gate, which is swung round, holding him against the side of the third corral, so that he is helpless and cannot fight or hurt himself while being branded or bridled.

Algernon chose a horse, and after he had been lunged on a lariat, Mr. Kerfoot saddled, mounted, and took him for a gallop over the prairie, and brought him in quite quiet. Unless a horse shows temper, this is about all the breaking he gets; constant work and plenty of it effect the rest.

Mrs. Kerfoot gave us a most excellent tea, with cakes of all kinds, which had been made by herself. Our ride home in the evening across the prairie was most enjoyable, the setting sun tipping the distant snowy peaks of the Rockies with golden and fiery red colours.

June 6th.—On the other side of the Bow river is a cañon known as "*the jumping pound*," over the edge of which the hunters used to drive the buffalo, and in this cañon their bones still lie in places two or three feet deep; they are now being taken away and used for manure.

A band of Blackfoot Indians passed to-day; the chief, "Three Plumes," rode up to the house to show his permit, which is given by the Indian agent to enable them to leave their reservations for a stated time; this band had been on a visit to the Stony Indians. We have since heard that the guests on leaving stole thirty ponies.

Had they passed here without showing their permit, the mounted police would have been informed, and it is one of their duties to see that the Indians remain on their reservations. They seemed very friendly, shook hands with all the men they saw about, inspected the railway engine with interest, and rode away. An Indian seldom expresses any surprise.

After the last rebellion several chiefs were taken to Montreal and shown everything that was calculated to impress them; the only remark they made was, "Why do not the white men make their squaws work?" Their squaws do all the hard work, but perhaps will have an easier time as the men get more civilized. In many cases there is a strong feeling of antipathy between the white and red men. The Indians in many parts of the North-West Territory bury their dead on a raised platform, the body is placed upon it wrapped in birch-bark, often with a piece of tobacco in the hand. I was sorry to hear that to get possession of this tobacco, the body is often pulled down by rough whites; and one can understand the distress this causes the Indians, whose dead are as sacred to them as ours are to us.

Whilst on their reservations they have a daily ration of food given to them, consisting of 1 lb. of meat, 1 lb. of flour, some tea and sugar; also one suit of clothes, a blanket, and $3 per annum.

June 7th.—Algernon and Tom C—— have gone into Calgary, which is twenty-five miles distant; they left at 7 A.M. and return to-morrow.

Adela and I took the ponies and drove in the buckboard

to see neighbours who have a cattle-ranch twelve miles from here. As we left the trail we bumped along over the prairie, but in this kind of carriage one does not feel it much, and finally found ourselves confronted by a large bog, which did not look inviting, but which appeared to be the only approach to the ranch. Adela went to inspect it accompanied by her faithful deer-hound Ginger. He sniffed the place suspiciously, but would not go through it; so after having wet her feet she was obliged to return to the buckboard, and finally after some trouble we drove through in safety, feeling much relieved when we found ourselves at the other side.

The ranche was a nice log-house, the inside being matchboarded with the red Douglas pine, which gave an air of comfort and refinement to the nicely-arranged rooms. The old Scotch lady and her two daughters were at home, and gave us an excellent tea, which we much enjoyed after our long drive. They do everything for themselves, having no servants, for the very good reason that on account of the loneliness of the place no one will stay with them.

I asked our hostess what had induced her to leave Scotland. She said her eldest son was one of the engineers on the C.P.R. and had advised her to come; that son was now married and had gone to Vancouver, so she and her daughters were now living with the younger son, who had just started this cattle-ranch.

It gives some idea of hardship when one sees ladies obliged to do everything for themselves. During the summer, when the days are long and sunny, it may be pleasant; I doubt it. But when the snow is deep, and the place shut off from all communication with the outer world, when the days close in at four o'clock, and wolves and bears occasionally prowl round the house, then these poor folk must wish themselves back again in their Highland home far over the wide sea.

June 11*th*.—Until this morning we have not seen the Rockies for nearly a week.

Innumerable wild flowers grow on the prairie; last month there were anemones of all colours, and in a few weeks there will be masses of dog-roses and wild honey-suckle: it is a kind provision of nature that this wild rose is so hardy, it stands even the extreme cold of winter, and grows from the root each year. The doctor, who is a botanist, sent a collection of wild flowers which he had made on the prairie to Kew Gardens, to be classified. He has lent me two books that I am glad to have: "Gray's Manual of Botany," and a catalogue of Canadian plants, by John McEwan, M.A., F.L.S., F.R.C.S.

One of the best districts for collecting wild flowers is at the foot of the Crowfoot valley; this place (and also Morley) are Indian reservations, and it is remarkable that in choosing them the Indians have selected the most fertile and prettiest valleys.

We went to see the coal-mine which was discovered three years ago; the first traces of coal being seen at the mouth of a badger's hole. Adela and I only went in as far as the end of the first gallery, where we met a man and horse bringing up a truck of coal to the mouth ; the others all departed along a similar gallery, each carrying a Davy lamp; as yet there is little danger of gas, the workings being quite near the surface.

June 13*th*.—I have become quite attached to all the animals here, and have undertaken the charge of the poultry; indeed I feel quite sorry for several of them, which have lost some of their toes from the effects of frost-bite: one old white hen runs about on stumps, seemingly not much inconvenienced! All the people here, who have poultry, find the necessity of keeping them very warm, and either make them "dug-outs" or else comfortable wooden houses. Eggs are still about 6s. a dozen, and chickens are almost impossible to procure. We have four chickens hatched, and four hens sitting.

Of other animals, "Ginger," the deer-hound, is a large tawny-coloured dog, and is supposed to be the last of his race, a descendant of Gelert; we have also "Jack," the kitchen dog, a thick-set brown spaniel, with a white chest, he has evidently been roughly treated at some time, as he is inclined to bite, and growls at every one ; his sole virtue is his devotion to the cook. When any one says "Go away, kitchen dog!" he struts off with his tail over his back. With one sitting-room, much confusion is caused by his appearance at lunch or dinner, as he and the deer-hound are on the worst of terms.

"Polly," a black retriever puppy, is so unaccustomed to

womankind, that when Adela or I go to play with her, she tries to escape by getting under the house, which is raised off the ground to make it dry during the winter, the ordinary way of building out here.

There are two pigs, a black and a white one; and two cows, a wild and a quiet one; and a calf which takes about three men to hold.

We shall soon be going "further west;" but our visit here has been a most pleasant one.

N—— made me a good easel to-day; he is a clever carpenter.

We saw a coyoté this evening. Two of the men crossed the river after him; but he was too wary to let them get a shot.

We heard last night of a Major ——, at Fort ——, who some years ago married a very beautiful squaw, a Blood Indian; he took her to England, and she has travelled with him to different places, and yet now, if she gets a chance, she throws off all her civilized dress, wraps herself in a blanket, and returns to her tribe. So wild are some of these races by nature, that civilized life for the first generation seems an impossibility.

June 16th.—We crossed the railway bridge over the Bow river; this was to me rather a difficult feat, as I had to walk on the sleepers and saw the river running beneath. In one of the railway cuttings we found a bed of fossilized mussels, and in the soil above we saw croppings of coal.

There is a wealth of grass all round us, such as one only

sees at home in the hay-time, and growing among it many
delightful wild flowers, most of them new to me.

June 18*th.*—Adela's sitting hens require a lot of running
after; half wild, and fleet as hares, they appear to have a
strange dislike to returning to their nests, so we have to
get some of the men to help us to run them down.

Two ranchers came to luncheon to-day—true types, I
should think, of "western men." I hear that their father
in England is a rich man, but he seems to do but little for
his sons. They work hard, even washing all their own
clothes and cooking, and it is not therefore to be wondered
at that they look rough.

The usual dress out here is a blue flannel shirt, with no
collar, but a coloured handkerchief tied loosely round the
neck, a buckskin shirt, a pair of leather "shaps" with fringes
down the seams, worn over trousers, boots, and a broad-
brimmed felt hat, with a leather band round it, which is
generally stamped with patterns and ornamented in some
way.

"Shap" is an abbreviation of the Mexican word "chap-
arajos," and are long leather leggings. A lariat coiled at
the horn of the Mexican saddle, a plaited leather bridle
with a severe Spanish bit, and a pair of smart spurs, often
silver-mounted, complete the cowboy's outfit. Further
south the saddle and bridle are often heavily plated with
silver; $300 and $400 is not an unusual price to pay for
them there, and though their owner is often short of
money, he will seldom part with these things.

Two men from a neighbouring ranche rode by this afternoon, they had been rounding up their cattle all day, and looked jaded and worn. We saw them drive out a refractory steer from a band of cattle which belonged to some one else,—no easy matter for them on their tired bronchos,—and after it was done they disappeared over the prairie, driving their steer in front of them.

June 19th to 20th.—Mr. Van Horne, president of the Canadian Pacific Railway, arrived by special train, and stayed for half-an-hour to talk over some business-matter with Mr. C——. He is on his way to Vancouver, and, I hear, generally goes at the rate of fifty miles an hour all through the mountains. His car is more like a house than a railway carriage, having bed-room, bath-room, dining-room, kitchen, and lastly, an excellent cook.

A good gallop over the prairie this morning was delightful. All the horses here are most excellent hacks, and never stumble.

June 21st.—To-day we visited the forest or timber limits, starting early. The ride was quite delightful, as we cantered up and down these limitless plains of grass, with the mountains stretching away into the dim distance as far as the eye could reach, and extending in Canada alone for 800 miles. I felt all the exhilaration that freedom gives in these untrodden solitudes. A horse must be ridden with a loose rein here, to enable him to see the gopher holes, of which the ground is full. Tares

INDIAN TEPÉS ON THE PRAIRIE.   [To face p. 48.

of many shades, pea-vine, wild camomile, cyclamens, bugle-flowers, and many other wild flowers, we saw as we rode along; also myrtles, gooseberries, and dog-roses. Occasionally a few prairie hen rose in front of us, and flew away, wondering doubtless at being disturbed.

As we came in view of the log-house where some of the lumbermen live, we saw the forest beneath us, and in the distance the snowy mountains; these great snow peaks change their aspect with every gleam of sunlight, with every shower, with every breath of wind, and in their ever-changing beauty continually suggested fresh thoughts from the book of Nature.

Lord Beaconsfield said that one might get tired of mountains, but that trees were a constant enjoyment; but I could never tire of the everlasting hills.

We rode on four miles further, over somewhat marshy ground, then, after descending a rather precipitous path, we found ourselves at a place which goes by the name of Dog Pond Creek; the horses were all picketed out, the harness and saddles having been removed.

We then went to fish in a pretty creek close by; the fish seemed amused by our efforts to catch them, for they moved slowly after the fly, but would not take; three times I changed it, but, alas! no luck.

Two nice Frenchwomen from the ranche near came to talk to us, and said it was useless, as the fish were only caught on a day with a bright sun shining. Mr. C—— then tried a minnow, with no better success; so we bundled up our rods, and wondered what we should do without fish for our luncheon.

Madame d'Artigue and her husband and sister (French people from the Basque Provinces) are in charge of this ranche for some one who lives in Calgary. It was quite a pleasure to see their beautifully-managed poultry-yards. There were hundreds of chickens of all ages and sizes, rows of boxes for the sitting hens with one hen in each, all arranged in the simple and practical manner peculiar to French people. There is an excellent market for poultry in the North-West; they told me that for a capon they got $1·75 cents in Calgary.

These good people were most hospitable, insisting on giving us a skim-milk cheese, a bucketful of milk, and a tin-dishful of eggs; with the last we made a large omelet, and with all these things, added to what we had brought from Mitford, made an excellent repast.

When the horses were being taken to water, four got loose, and galloped off, much to our dismay; but Tom C—— on his excellent cow pony soon brought them back again. We said good-bye to the kind-hearted French people, who stood waving their hands to us, until a rising mound hid them from our sight. Continuing our ride, we stopped and had tea at the I——'s. We were all rather tired, and the mosquitoes were very troublesome this evening, literally covering the horses, but fortunately annoying us less by their bites than by their numbers.

Sunday, June 24th.—In the evening we had a service

from a travelling minister—about half the men came; the hymns selected by him were not at all cheerful nor bright, and his sermon was not suitable in any way to the requirements of his listeners, which one regretted.

Two hens hatched off to-day twenty-six chickens, a welcome addition to the poultry-yard; and, as Adela and I have taken much trouble, we felt rewarded.

Algernon rode to the horse-ranch, and, as we leave to-morrow, he returned the horse kindly lent to him.

Rather a tragic termination to our visit was caused by another accident on the railway. In the evening we heard the mill-whistle blowing violently, and found that the engine, returning with four trucks of lumber, had been thrown off the rails; the engineer got jammed between the engine and the logs, and had his leg broken in two places; but such is the toughness of these men that when being carried down we heard him joking with the others about not yet needing to be carried feet first, though he must have been suffering great pain.

CHAPTER V.

BANFF—GOOD FISHING IN MINNEWONKA LAKE.

"Lo—peak on peak in stairways sit
In stepping-stones that reach to God."

June 26th.—Said good-bye to the C——s last night with regret. A train which stops to take up passengers at 3 A.M. is unusual at home, but such was the hour at which we left Mitford, and we reached Banff at 7 A.M. We did not think a sleeping-car necessary, as it was only a four hours' journey, and we were rewarded, on entering the Rockies at Canmore at early dawn, by the rare beauty of the sunrise.

The large hotel of the Canadian Pacific Railway Company at Banff is built entirely of wood, like an enormous Swiss châlet; it stands alone, about half a mile from the small but rapidly growing town.

The hotel has accommodation for 300 persons; it is exceedingly comfortable in every respect. Wonderful enterprise on the part of the Company to have erected such a fine building in the middle of these mountains!

June 27th.—We got a capital suite of rooms with a lovely view, for 3½ dollars a day. This included everything except wine.

A glorious day was our first here. In the afternoon we went in a steam-launch up the Bow river, some young Englishmen having started two of these boats as a speculation. We went in one called the "Mountain Belle," the only other passengers being two elderly people on their way to England from Australia, who were spending a few days at the hotel. The scenery was magnificent, and at each bend of the river we saw something new and pleasing. The water was of an intensely green colour, caused by the number of glacier streams which poured into it. The young woods looked bright and green, but the burnt trunks of fallen giant trees, told of the terrible bush fires which have run through these woods in past times.

In all directions were seen strips of burnt timber, extending from the base of the mountains to the snow-line, showing where the fires have run up to the mountain tops through the green woods. Snowy peaks reared their ragged crests into the sky on all sides. Among such scenes we passed up the river for twelve miles, though, owing to the sandbanks shifting, there was some difficulty in the navigation, but our skipper seemed to know his business.

We then disembarked at a little moss-covered shanty, which has been built as a restaurant for the summer months, and sat on the banks surveying the loveliness around.

All the little streams which run into the Bow river near here are full of trout which take a fly greedily.

I was the first lady who had been so far up the river.

June 20th.—We hired a couple of bronchos and rode to the Minnewonka Lake. In the Indian language Minnewonka means "The bad spirit," but I am sorry to say the settlers often call it the "devil's lake," which is a very ugly name compared with the Indian one.

In the same way they have changed the names of many of the mountains—for the worse I think, as those chosen by the Indians were always much more appropriate.

Our first start was not promising; a very lame pony came for one of us, and some time was spent in exchanging this for another; and though Algernon got a good one, mine was a real bone-shaker, and was so tired that I could hardly keep him on his legs. This was not quite what we had wished with a nine-mile ride before us, but sometimes one's mood is to make the best of everything, and the beauty of the scene soon made me forget my miserable steed. At one moment we were galloping across grassy flats, then through wooded valleys. with ranges of high mountains as far as we could see in every direction, and as we kept ascending we saw the river winding away among the woods far below. In one of the prettiest places we passed was a large camp of Stony Indians, and we were greeted by a mob of Indian dogs, which ran out barking and snapping at our ponies.

The Stonies are now a very peaceable people, and many

of them are Methodists. At their reservation at Morley is a large Methodist mission.

Though the white men are not allowed to shoot game until August 15th, the Indians have no restrictions of this kind, and therefore the destruction of game with them goes on in season and out of season.

We were now in the burnt woods, and, the trail being very rough, had to go slowly. Upon the grass slopes of Castle Mountain, which stood high above us, are sometimes to be seen the Rocky Mountain goat; and a black bear in search of berries may also be descried occasionally, but we saw none and pursued our way.

The trail has been improved in the last two years, so that a carriage can jolt along to the lake; but I pity the poor sufferers inside. Originally it was an Indian trail winding about in all directions.*

Occasionally we crossed a log bridge over a creek. As we went along I observed many wild flowers growing by the side of the trail, especially a red Castilleia growing in great bushes, and columbines of every shade and hue.

Having reached the lake about 6 A.M., we found two log-houses in course of building, and after some little trouble secured one of the workers to go out fishing with us. We unsaddled the ponies, and having watered them at the lake, picketed them with the lariat one always carries in this country, among the best grass we could see, and left them eating it and the pea-vine, which the horses love better than anything.

* Since writing this a good new road has been made from Banff.

We started in an excellent boat which our man had just built, and rowed gently down the lake ; but, alas, it was not possible to catch these trout with the rods we had brought. Our boatman told us the lake was 600 feet deep, and the fish were generally lying just off the shallow places, so we were reluctantly obliged to troll with a spoon. We got into a nice bay out of the wind, and the bright sun made everything look pleasant.

Algernon suddenly said, " I've got one;" the line was slowly drawn in, and we awaited the arrival of the fish in breathless suspense. " Are you sure he is there ? " " Is he a big one ? " were the questions which quickly followed ; (the fish, big or small, came along slowly) Algernon was getting towards the end of the line, two sinkers had already been drawn into the boat, the boatman got ready his gaff. " Here he comes," said Algernon, "a big one, by Jove ! " Although he had come pretty quietly he did not like the look of the boat, gave a sudden roll, the line snapped, he was off—no, gaffed just two inches above the tail, and he was thrown into the boat with a heavy flop, a 28-lb. trout, measuring three feet in length and over ten inches in depth. We congratulated ourselves that the fish was with us instead of in the lake, and having mended the line and fixed the spoon, prepared for another try. Not so fast. We rowed about for some time without a nibble, and although the fish did not take, we had a pleasant time, and kept hoping our luck would change. For what is life worth without hope, which gives zest to the true sportsman, who with it is content with little, sometimes, nay often, with nothing.—Hope carries us poor mortals cheerfully on from the cradle to the grave ; and though, perhaps, through some fault in ourselves, what we wish to attain turns out a "Will of the Wisp," still one always goes on cheerfully looking for better things.

But to return to our fishing. We became hungry, and, having brought nothing with us, landed at the boatman's "shack," where he quickly lighted a fire, and made us some excellent tea, and with bread, jam, and biscuits we managed pretty well. We hoped to have added fish to our feast, but had it not in our hearts to cut up the big one at once, as we wished to show him at the hotel.

After having a look at the ponies we started again in the boat, and by six o'clock had landed three more fish, weighing respectively three, four, and six pounds. With a nine-mile ride before us we felt it was time to start for the hotel, and having resaddled, the question arose, what was to be done with the spoil. We did not wish to leave it behind, and if we did not pack it with us, there was no other means of getting it home. So Algernon wrapped up the big fish in a sack, which he tied firmly to the back of his Californian saddle, and the other three, secured in the same way, were fastened with buckskin thongs to my saddle. Off we started for the hotel, but the transit of the fish was not so easy a matter; several times Algernon had to stop and retie the thongs, and still they flopped about and were uncomfortable baggage; not until 8.30 did we reach our destination, tired and hot after our long day. Several people came to see our fish at the door, amongst them oné enthusiastic fisherman—of course, English—who quickly brought scales, and weighed the biggest. " A good twenty-eight pounds ! " he said.

We were glad to eat our dinner—the chef serving the fish as " Truite à la St. Maur "—and even more so to turn into a good bed.

June 29*th*.—Connor, the forester of the National Park here, took us for a long ride; we had two excellent ponies, which "loped" along with us as if they had nothing on their backs; of course my weight was insignificant, but Algernon, with his Californian saddle, which weighs 35 lbs., must ride 17 stone.

The National Park, which the Government is making here, is a tract of country about twenty-eight miles square, including some grand mountains and splendid scenery, amongst which they are laying out roads and riding-paths, and in this park they hope to preserve the various game animals of the country ; but for the latter purpose the size is inadequate. We received every kindness and civility from the Superintendent of the Park—Mr. Stewart, who lives in a nice log-house near to the Canadian Pacific Railway Hotel.

The Stony Indians killed two mountain sheep close to Lake Minnewonka a day or two ago. The Rocky Mountain Sheep, or American Big-Horn (*Ovis montana*), has a coat of hair like that of a deer, or still more like a caribou; a large ram stands as high as 3 ft. 6 in. in the shoulder, and weighs over 300 lbs. There is a splendid specimen of a head at Mr. Stewart's office, which was shot by the forester last winter. These creatures are exceedingly timid, choosing the most inaccessible places as feeding-grounds; being great climbers, and able to jump from enormous heights, they can often evade the hunters when pursued, and this makes their heads one of the most valued trophies of the Western hunter.

We rode along with our guide for five or six miles on the same trail as yesterday, and after picketing the ponies, turned off sharp to the right, and walked over very rough ground covered with burnt timber, to a cañon which Connor said he had just discovered. We climbed over the large charred logs, which was not a very clean amusement, for a few hundred yards, and then entered the cañon, which I can better describe as a deep ravine, almost closing over our heads, with precipitous rocks on either side, not unlike the eerie places which are occasionally seen in some wild Highland glen. The shades of the big pine trees somewhat darkened the cañon, still we were able to admire the lovely mosses and lichens which grew in the richest profusion among the fallen timber.

As it seemed to me probable that we might come across a bear, and as none of us had brought even a revolver, I declined to go further; for in such a place it would have been impossible to run away, for we could only go slowly over the windfalls, and a bear visited thus in his own stronghold might resent intrusion. On our way in, Connor had shown us a place where he had seen one only three weeks before. Bears are extremely fond of fruit and berries of all kinds, and, when in season, these creatures are generally found where they are growing in any quantity. Early in the morning and just before sundown are the best times to find bear.

We got back for a late dinner, and in the evening heard Liszt's 2nd Rhapsodie, beautifully played by an American lady on the new Steinway grand piano in the music-room; a treat hardly to be expected in the middle of the Rockies.

June 30*th*.—A very early start and a delightful morning ride brought us again to Lake Minnewonka, where we fished all day. We had a fair wind and sailed, which enabled us to get much further than last time, and had another excellent day's fishing.

Our bag of Thursday weighed 42 lbs., this day's fifteen fish weighed 51 lbs.; we got one fine trout of 12 lbs., two of 8 lbs., and the rest from 6 to 4 lbs. We lunched about eight miles down the lake, at a very pretty place with a shingly beach and nicely-timbered bank. Our boatman (by the way, a gentleman), who, for some reason best known to himself, had chosen this rough life, had thoughtfully brought cups, plates, knives, tea and a kettle; and as we had plenty of trout, and a good fire, we soon had some cooked, and enjoyed an excellent lunch. The Indian manner of cooking fish we found best; the fish is split down the middle, boned and stretched out like a kipper on a long split stick, the lower end of which is stuck into the ground; the fish is placed lengthways, and the upper end of the split is then secured with a strip of bark. The skin side is turned to the fire, and left to broil, and the fish is afterwards, if large, turned, and the other side treated in the same way; but with a small fish, cooking on one side is sufficient.

I never could understand how it was, that though I often saw the Indians cooking fish without salt, when done they seemed not to require any. Was it for the reason that hunger was the best sauce, or that being freshly out of the water, the flavour of the fish was so good that it required nothing to improve it?

I found tea also was much more palatable without milk than I would have imagined: when no luxuries can be had, one soon learns to do without them, and the people who live on hardy fare seem contented enough.

To-day, however, we met an exception in a rough-looking miner, who hailed from Barnsley in Yorkshire. As we were nearing the shore of the lake after our day's fishing, we heard a considerable flow of language, not of the choicest, emanating from the interior of the log shanty where our boatman lived. The latter explained that the miner there was a "rough lot," and that we had better leave him alone: on landing, however, we were surprised to find that the said rough customer had taken the trouble to bring in and saddle our ponies. We thanked him and talked to him for a few minutes; he told me that he had been in two bad colliery explosions since arriving in Canada, and had come to the Lake to rest and recover from the effects of them. He had been six years in the Dominion, but said that, when he got to work again, he hoped to save $100 and go home to Barnsley. "In the old country," he said, "when sick, we are well looked after; in Canada we are well paid while we can work, but if we get ill, no one cares."

He took off his hat, and showed us he had hardly any hair, it had all been burnt off at the colliery accident at Nanaimo in Vancouver Island, where fifty Chinamen were killed, this poor fellow saving his life by climbing up a rope in the air-shaft.

I said to him, "No pay would compensate me for passing so much of my time in the dark." "Oh," he answered, "we boys like it," and we parted.

July 1st, Sunday.—Algernon and I went to church, and joined in the English service in the Methodist Chapel.

In Canada there is a heavy fine for any one compelling another to work on Sunday. The Canadian Pacific trains do not leave Vancouver or Montreal on that day, though those that have started previously continue their journey.

July 2nd.—Algernon and a man from this hotel went off to try and get a bear to-day. They returned in the evening tired out after a tremendous walk over the mountains, having only seen a porcupine, which they shot on the roof of an old lumber-camp they found in the valley the other side of the mountains they had crossed over.

The following extracts were quoted to us by Dr. H., who was a long while in the employ of the Hudson's Bay

Company. There were many interesting entries in the old Hudson's Bay Company's journals and entry-books kept at the different forts; but some years ago most of the oldest books were unfortunately destroyed.

"Dec. 31st, 1795. Served out a quart of rum per man; the evening spent in innocent mirth and jollity.

"Jan. 1st, 1796. All the Indians drunk about the place, great trouble in keeping order."

The following entry appears even of an earlier date, and must have come from the far north.

"The Company's cook, a lad of 16, having been carried off by the Esquimaux, three out of a party of six passing Esquimaux were seized as hostages until the return of the boy."

Here there was a break of five years in the journal, and it did not state if he was recovered: probably not, from the following:—" Had a row with the three Esquimaux detained. They were shot, and their ears pickled in rum, and sent on to their tribe, to show them what had happened."

This treatment appears somewhat harsh, but retributive justice overawes savages as nothing else has power to do.

To the Hudson's Bay Company we owe a debt of gratitude, for they were the pioneers of civilization in the North-West. They were the first to open up an organized system of trade in this wild region, and always dealt honestly with the Indians, keeping good stores, and by just dealing earned their respect.

At the earliest fur sales, the bidding was done, as it was

called, "by the candle." As each bale of furs was put up to auction a candle was lighted, and the person bidding last, as the candle went out, got the furs. The candle burnt about two minutes.

July 3rd.—News from Montreal brings the intelligence of 30 deaths from sunstroke; also of intense heat in Manitoba, with a temperature of 105°. Here the weather is quite delightful, even a little chilly in the evening.

The Indian legend of Lake Minnewonka runs thus: One of the first Indians who saw this lake did so by climbing to the top of one of the highest mountains which surrounded it. In the lake he saw an enormous fish, so large that from where he stood it looked the whole length of the lake, to which he therefore gave its present name, The Lake of the Evil Spirit.

Near Banff there are five hot sulphur springs; the two principally used flow from the central spur of Sulphur Mountain, 800 feet above the level of Bow river; the main spring issues at the rate of a million and a half gallons daily, and has a temperature of 115°. A short way from it there is another, with a temperature of 85°. Round these springs have lately been erected small bathing-houses, where hot baths can be obtained, the water being brought in pipes from the springs; a quarter-dollar is charged for a bath. I heard that, besides sulphur, iron and thirteen other substances occur in this water, and that it is specially beneficial in rheumatism and skin diseases. We saw a pair of crutches hanging up

THE BOW RIVER. [*To face p.* 64.

in the trees. On a board below was printed, "The owner of these has left the springs—cured!"

Half a mile from Banff are more hot springs, one in a large cave; the only entrance to it used to be by a funnel-shaped hole in the roof, through which people were lowered by a rope; this has now been improved by an opening from the side through a gallery. In this natural chamber is a pool 30 feet wide where the water comes bubbling up; however, the fumes of sulphur are too strong to be pleasant. A few yards from this is the Basin, a large plunge bath in the open, surrounded by overhanging rocks. Here most of the visitors to Banff enjoy a swim. Very hot sulphur baths should not be taken without the advice of a doctor, as they have a lowering effect on the action of the heart; here, as in other places, we met persons suffering from the abuse of them.

There are two neat Swiss châlets built at the cave and basin, containing dressing-rooms; tea can be obtained in them, and as they are only half a mile from the town, they are most accessible, and consequently most popular with tourists.

The Banff Hotel is lighted by electricity, but under the present management it is turned off at ten o'clock; a most awkward custom this proved, as we were in the midst of packing for a start at 5 A.M. when out went the lights. We fortunately got candles, which helped us through our difficulties.

CHAPTER VI.

Vancouver—Victoria.

" Primeval forests! virgin sod!
That Saxon has not ravished yet."—*Joaquin Miller.*

July 4th.—Left Banff at an early hour before daylight. The clerk at the station was very troublesome about our saddles; said they must follow us. We afterwards found there would have been no difficulty in checking them to Vancouver with the other baggage had we put them into a packing-case with handles—a useful thing to know. The system of checking baggage through to its destination, which is in general use all through Canada and the States, is excellent and saves much trouble. You hand your luggage over, and receive checks in exchange. On presenting these at the end of your journey, you receive your belongings.

The morning was lovely, with a few showers, which made the mountains more than ever grand. The words of the Canticle kept recurring to me: "O ye mountains and hills, bless ye the Lord! praise Him and magnify Him for over!" On leaving Banff for Vancouver, the railway runs alongside the Bow river, and through well-timbered valleys. On the left lie the Vermilion Lakes, where there is good trout-fishing, and in the distance is seen Mount Massive and the snow peaks of many others of the range. On we go, past Castle Mountain, which towers above us in one sheer precipice of 5,000 feet, and the further we travel in this direction the more grand and impressive the scenery becomes. Many people obtain a permit to ride on the cow-catcher of the engine. We were contented to look at the scenery from the platform of the car, and for this purpose we had camp-stools placed outside.

While we made the ascent to the station called Stephen, an extra engine of enormous power was attached behind us; thus we reached the summit of the Rocky Mountains.

All the gradients on the Canadian Pacific Railway which exceed 1 in 100 are concentrated on the 134 miles from the Bow river, three miles east of the summit of the Rockies, to the Albert Cañon on the Illecillewast. From Stephen the line descends rapidly, passing the beautiful Wapta Lake, and crossing the deep ravine of the same name, now more commonly known as the Kicking-Horse Pass. The scenery here is almost terrible in its grandeur; and as we rushed along, we could only marvel at the triumphs of engineering skill which have enabled men to overcome the tremendous difficulties of constructing a railway through this place. High over our heads we see many grand mountains, the highest peaks of which are hidden from our view by snow and mist, while far below rushes the mountain torrent. The Cañon rapidly deepens, till beyond Palliser the mountain sides become vertical, rising straight up thousands of feet. Down this vast chasm the railway and river go together. Ledges are cut out of the solid rock, and the track crosses and re-crosses the ravine, turning and twisting in every direction.

On leaving the Rockies behind us, we passed through the little mining-town of Golden City, situated near the Columbia river.

An excellent steamer runs up this river for eighty miles to the Columbia lakes. It is a pleasant trip, and only takes three or four days; and in late autumn the lagoons along the river-side are the haunts of thousands of wild-fowl.

From Golden City the range of the Selkirk Mountains extends in an apparently unbroken line from the S.W. to the N.E. Near here is the oldest log-camp in the Mountains, where a Government engineering party, under Mr. Walter Moberly, C.E., spent the winter of 1871.

I classed our journey from Banff to Vancouver into three interesting divisions. Each was beautiful, but entirely different.

1st. The Kicking-Horse Pass and the Rocky Mountains.

2nd. The passes through the Selkirk Mountains, and the views of the Great Glacier.

3rd. The Cañons and valley of the Fraser river.

The last-named is supposed to be one of the finest salmon rivers in the world, though, to a sportsman, it is a disappointing fact that the salmon here will not take a fly.

From Golden the line gradually ascends at the rate of 116 feet to the mile, and soon the Columbia river is left 1,000 feet below. The mountain sides here are densely timbered with enormous trees; the great size of the Douglas pine, spruce, and cedars was surprising.

The finest of all the mountain peaks along the line is the one named Sir Donald, which seemed to rear its rocky and vast pinnacles close against the sky.

The principal difficulties in the construction of this part of the line were caused by the mountain torrents rushing down through narrow gorges, over which the trains had to pass by bridging, snow-sheds, or tunnelling.

The highest of these bridges is crossed at Stony Creek, it is 295 feet above the water, and the highest bridge in the world, and is constructed entirely of timber. There are over six miles of snow-sheds in the Selkirks. Without these the line could not be kept open in winter, on account of the avalanches, or "snow-slides," as they are called here.

As we neared the "Glacier House," we had our first glimpse of the Great Glacier, which looks like an immense river of ice; but although it is enormous, several of those in Switzerland are larger.

A good hotel has been built here by the Canadian Pacific Railway Company.

We continued the descent from this place, and the loop was soon reached, where the line made several startling twists and turns, first crossing a valley leading from the

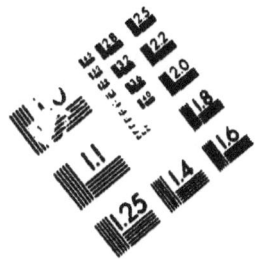
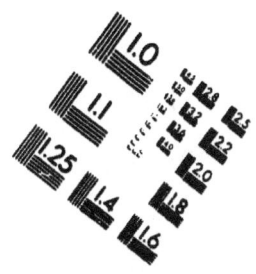

**IMAGE EVALUATION
TEST TARGET (MT-3)**

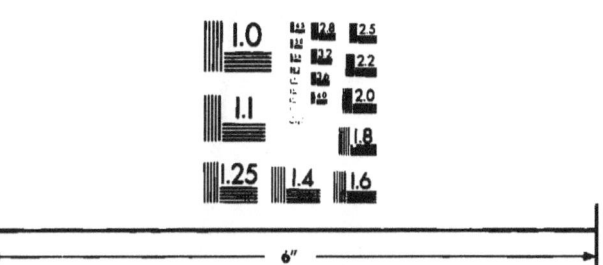

Photographic
Sciences
Corporation

23 WEST MAIN STREET
WEBSTER, N.Y. 14580
(716) 872-4503

Ross Peak Glacier, then touching for a moment on Ross Peak; and from there doubling back upon itself. The construction of the engine and carriage wheels of American railways render these sharp curves practicable, and they have these loops now on many other railways in the States. We saw lovely flowers and shrubs on the rugged slopes of some of the deep ravines, and in several of the mountain valleys red lilies, columbines in endless variety, waving ferns, strange grasses, hemlocks, and bulrushes.

A missionary with his sick wife joined the cars at a place called Field, and the whole of the following day she was lying with the curtains drawn across her bed, in the same car in which we were all travelling. Later, at one of the stations where we stopped, a doctor came to see her, but, owing to the short time the train remained there, he could do little for her. The husband took refuge in tears, and seemed utterly overcome by his troubles. I felt sorry for them. First warning them that I was not a lady doctor, I offered to see his wife. She was a poor, nervous, hysterical woman, very ill certainly, but not dying, as she supposed. A little cheering up did wonders. I wanted medicine; none was at hand. Fortunately I remembered Algernon had in one of his bags a bottle of castor oil of rough quality for softening the leather of his boots. I dosed the poor lady with this! and before they left she was certainly better.

I have always been told three things are safe to try in case of illness: 1st, hot bath; 2nd, a dose; 3rd, put the patient to bed.

The husband was a Methodist minister, and they were on their way to Cariboo for mission work among the miners there, when she was taken ill. They had been at Field for a fortnight, and were now coming by train in order to be near a doctor. They were both extremely helpless people; he looked ridiculously young, and she physically unfitted for the wild and comfortless life she had before her. Some people have such powers of mind that they rise above all bodily weakness, and cannot be hindered by physical infirmity from anything they undertake. She, poor soul! was not one of these fortunate characters.

The helpless are always to be pitied, and are, I am sorry to say, looked down upon by working men who can "turn their hands to anything."

One suggestion I would like to make to the directors of the Canadian Pacific Railway Company, that in the interests of the majority there is absolute necessity to provide separate accommodation for sick persons. To travel for days with sick and suffering people (as we had to do more than once) who would fain have quiet, and cannot stand the least noise or motion, is hard on every one. The difficulty, I fear, will remain unsolved if extra payment is required, as many invalids would be unable to pay more than for a sleeping carriage.

Gangs of Chinese labourers were at work on the line, and we passed their little camps, where little rickety tents held aloft by a few sticks of bamboo seemed their only shelter. In these camps thirty or forty men live, subsisting principally on rice and a little dried fish, quite content so long as they are making enough money with which to return to their own country. They are excellent labourers, very industrious and, as a rule, honest, working for lower wages than the white men. This is one of the many reasons why there is such a strong feeling against them. They lower the rate of wages in a country where they get a footing. Nearly all the domestic servants at Vancouver and in Victoria are Chinese. People living here told me they did not know what they should do without them, and in Victoria they have their own quarter in the city.

All along the Cañon of the Fraser river reminded me of the scenery in the Highlands of Scotland on a large scale.

The railway seemed often to run on trestles of wood fastened to the solid rock, which often goes in one sheer precipice down to the rushing river below, the water of which appeared a mud colour.

We had glimpses of Indians fishing for salmon from time to time; sitting in their dug-out canoes, they looked picturesque. The salmon they smoke and dry for their winter food.

The train passed through many tunnels, and when at last the old and nearly deserted town of Yale was reached, we felt we were getting near the end of our journey. Formerly this was an important place, the head of navigation on the Fraser river; and from it by the old government road, which followed the course of the river, the Cariboo and other mining districts were reached.

Now the railway has changed everything, and consequently many nice-looking little wooden houses, with their patches of garden, are closed and deserted. A feeling of sadness came over me at the sight of pretty little desolate homes. The apple and cherry trees, of which there were many, were in full bloom, and the rich green colouring of the valley, with the broad river flowing through it, gave an appearance of prosperity which in reality did not exist; for, the moment the railway took the trade from the place, the inhabitants migrated.

After Yale was left behind, we passed into more open country, and seemed to be continually crossing creeks and lagoons, which, with the sunshine of early morning on them, looked lovely. Then as we approached Vancouver, we came into heavily-timbered country, and at last reached the terminus of the Canadian Pacific Railway, Vancouver.

In May 1886, the site of this town was occupied by dense forest, the trees being of enormous size. During the two following months a clearing was made, and a town built; in July of that same year it was entirely destroyed by fire, one house alone remaining. With the usual energy of the "western man," the following day building was recommenced. Vancouver now has a population of 5,000 people; there is an excellent harbour, and a regular steamship service to Victoria, Vancouver Island, China, Japan, San Francisco, Alaska, and Puget Sound Ports. Land has already become of great value in the town of Vancouver, and in a few years it will be an important place.

We went on board the steamer *Yosemité* here; after the usual delay in getting our luggage, we steamed off for Victoria, Vancouver Island, which is 80 miles distant. It seems rather stupid to have called the new town, which is the terminus of the railway, by the same name as the island, as it must sometimes lead to confusion.

The sea was like a mirror, and therefore I was able to enjoy the beautiful scenery. As we left the harbour, we saw on our left the range of high mountains, known as the Coast range, the peaks of which were still white with snow; splendid forests stretched in every direction, and as these were left behind, we passed numbers of prettily-wooded islands.

Far to the south, in American territory, the peak of Mount Baker, 13,000 feet, rears its solitary, cone-like crest into the sky; 3,000 feet of this mountain are covered with perpetual snow.

We arrived about sunset at Victoria, and were surprised with the smallness of the harbour; the best harbour on the island is at Esquimault, a few miles north of Victoria.

July 7th, Dryad Hotel, Victoria.—Instead of housemaids here Chinamen do the work, and do it very well too, except that they have an awkward way of rushing into the rooms without knocking; but as I had an inner room only accessible through Algernon's, this did not affect me much. It seemed odd at first not to be able to ask the Chinamen for what was wanted, but there was a set of diminutive boys called "bellboys," who seemed able to make them understand.

We went for a long drive, visiting the dry dock at Esquimault, but I am persuaded that our Jehu, for some reason of his own, kept going round and round, perhaps by way of lengthening our pleasure and his remuneration ! The carriages are heavy lumbering landaus. I find many are sent out from England, the inside being filled with goods, and the wheels being also put inside. No doubt they are unsaleable at home, and they are got rid of in this way.

Victoria is a quiet little place, with many nice houses standing in their own gardens. Honeysuckle grows in the greatest profusion up the sides of the houses, and in festoons over the verandahs. The native honeysuckle is the red variety; but, in Victoria, where they prefer everything English, they have planted the sweet-smelling English kind, which now grows most luxuriantly everywhere.

There is a cathedral here, and many churches of other denominations. The Bishop of Victoria is at present in England. We went to see his garden, which is one of the prettiest in the place. Mrs. Hills, the Bishop's wife, took the greatest interest in it, but she died some months ago. A brown retriever sat howling piteously on the door-step of the house, and we were told that ever since her death this poor faithful animal had thus mourned the loss of his mistr 's in this way !

There is a fine hospital at Victoria, entirely managed

by Roman Catholics. Another large one is now being built for the Protestants of this place. We saw also the house of the Roman Catholic Archbishop, who has just been murdered.

The coal here, and in fact all down the Pacific coast, is supplied from the mines at Nanaimo. Mr. Dunsmuir,* who now owns these mines, began life as a labouring man. His career reads like a fairy tale :—Returning from work one evening, he found the indications of coal. Being too poor to develop the mine himself, he waited, and ultimately found two Englishmen ready to invest £10,000 apiece in the enterprise. He soon bought them out, and now possesses the whole mine, from which he has realized an enormous fortune. He has been exceedingly generous with his money, and is greatly respected, and is virtually the builder and owner of the only railway in the island—that from Victoria to Nanaimo.

Sunday, July 8th.—A glorious summer day. We went to St. John's Church, which is no distance from the hotel, and thoroughly appreciated the service after having been out of reach of a church for weeks. The rector, the Rev. J. Jenns, gave us most excellent sermons both morning and evening, and from him and others we received much attention and kindness.

July 9th.—We walked up to the barracks in the morning. Colonel Holmes and Major Peters showed us

* He has died since we were in Victoria.

everything of interest in the place. A battery of artillery is stationed here. I asked to see the medals some of the men wore; they were given after the last half-breed rebellion, which was headed by Riel, who was afterwards hanged—a fate he richly deserved.

At Fish Creek, where one of the principal engagements took place, twenty out of the sixty men in this battery were killed. The Indians—more especially the Blackfeet and Bloods—are great warriors when they get on the war-path, so that this rebellion would have been much more serious if the Indians had joined the half-breeds. It was in a great measure prevented by the cowboys, who told the Indians that if they went on the war-path they would shoot down their women and children. This had the effect of keeping them quiet. The power of the Indians is now pretty well broken, as they have so many intertribal quarrels that they seldom or never combine, and without combination can do little harm to the rapidly increasing settlers.

The Indians along the coast make a good living by catching salmon in the salt water with the spoon, and at certain seasons they can be caught in this way in the harbour of Esquimault, and give good sport.

July 11*th*.—Mr. T——, who arrived here last night, Algernon, and I started on a fishing expedition to the Cowichan Lake. In a useful little note-book which Algernon treasures, we find this entry: "When in Vancouver Island, be sure and try Cowichan Lake for salmon."

We had procured our provisions and a tent from the Hudson Bay Stores here. We left Victoria early in the morning by train, and after two or three hours' journey got off at a station called Duncan, after the first settler, who came here twenty-six years ago—a nice old man, with a pleasant wife. He had engaged Indians for us, and done all he could to start us comfortably.

While we were packing our luggage on the waggon at Duncan, one of the horses was much terrified when he winded a bear. Two men could hardly hold him, and until we started he shivered with fright. No doubt the power of scenting danger is a great protection to animals who would be otherwise helpless.

The bear which caused all this alarm was not very formidable—no larger than a spaniel. An Indian had brought him in from the woods a few weeks before, and a funny little fellow he was, so droll in his movements. He ran about all over the place, seeming greatly to enjoy a game of romps with the dogs. A squaw brought a pailful of berries to sell; some were given to him. He was so much afraid that the dogs would take them that he say down, encircling them with his paws, and devoured them with the greatest haste. When he found that the pail had gone to the kitchen, he made three sudden raids in that direction, but each time was circumvented by his owner. He was very mischievous, and climbed like a cat. We saw him run up a scaffolding-pole, which reached above the second floor of the hotel, with the greatest ease. Black bears, of which this was one, climb well. They are not so savage as grizzlies, for the former will seldom attack a man unless wounded.

We jolted along in our waggon through the most beautiful woods I had ever seen. The great cedar-trees towered far above us, and also magnificent specimens of the Douglas pine and spruce. We felt glad that the lumbermen with their relentless axes had not yet disturbed the harmony of the place. Here and there we saw where a tree had been felled to make room for a waggon to pass on the trail.

Our driver told us that once after a storm he had found no less than thirty-five fallen trees across the trail; when we see their size, we understand the labour entailed in chopping. Of course, when the trail was cleared after the storm, many of them were not disturbed, but the track was carried round them.

We were told of a tree near Cowichan Lake 89 feet in circumference, but we did not see it, and rather doubt its existence. In the forest fires the Douglas pine does not suffer so much as other trees, owing to the great thickness of its bark. The trunks are often charred and blackened, but still the tree grows in great luxuriance. In the marshes and swampy grounds of these woods is found a great leafy plant which is called by the settlers skunk cabbage, of which bears are extremely fond. When they emerge from their winter sleep, they search for and devour it greedily. When the hybernating season is over, these animals are in good condition, but a few weeks afterwards they become extremely thin.

Mountain lion, lynx, and deer of several varieties are also found in these woods, and in winter a great many timber-wolves. Tree-grouse also abound; they are somewhat larger than the Scotch grouse, perch in the trees, and if alarmed, when on the ground, run, but if in a tree, they remain perfectly still while one approaches within a few yards of them, evidently trusting to their colour for concealment. On this account they are commonly known by the name of "fool hens." In Canada there are no less than five varieties of this beautiful bird.*

Some parts of the trail were very rough. The pole bent like a bow as our waggon jolted down some of the steep gulches. This looked alarming; but in the wilds one thinks little of these things, and becomes accustomed to all kinds of tracks and modes of transit. Often we had to hold on tight to prevent being jerked off the waggon over stumps and cahôts (holes).

Physical weakness and infirmities are hard to bear in all places, but those who are delicate and unwilling to rough it, should not attempt difficult expeditions in this country; great energy and an utter disregard for the comforts of life are required the moment the beaten track is left; but for the strong, healthy, and vigorous, camping out means rest and enjoyment; troubles seem left far behind, while one lives from day to day in close contact with the beauties of nature; and I cannot but feel that many

* 1. Cock of the Plains—*Tetrao (centrocercus) urophasianus.* 2. Dusky grouse—*Tetrao obscurus.* 3. Sharp-tailed grouse—*Tetrao (centrocercus) Phasianellus.* 4. Ruff grouse—*Tetrao umbellus.* 5. Pinnated grouse.

men worn out with sedentary work in large cities would have their nerves and bodies invigorated were they to try a month or two of repose in these vast solitudes, instead of remaining at their post until health is utterly destroyed.

We had been told we should find an hotel near Cowichan Lake; we did find a log-house, but with little in it, so dirty and comfortless we did not care to remain there; so having procured the loan of a boat, as our canoes were not to arrive until the morrow, we put our kit into it, and rowed to seek a camping-ground.

By this time evening was closing in, and my first experience of camping was rather a rough one; the brushwood was so thick that we had to "swamp it" out with an axe; when this was done, the tent up, and the fire lighted, things looked better, though to me the place appeared weird and chill in the evening light; to Algernon it was nothing, he having spent years in the woods in times gone by.

The sun, which had thrown a flood of golden light over everything, now disappeared, leaving us in the ever-increasing darkness to make the best arrangements we could for the night.

My advice to campers-out is, to be prepared for every inconvenience, for, however complete are the arrangements, generally something is forgotten; make the best of it, feeling it is but a shifting scene in the great drama of life, and though this camping-ground is damp, and overgrown with bush, and there is an ominous and disturbing buzzing of insects, to-morrow's camp may be dry and delightful.

G

The first misfortune happened to a large glass bottle of home-made raspberry jam, which the good woman at the hotel at Duncan, had allowed us to buy, after seeing it made. This slipped from my hands whilst I was getting out of the boat, and the bottle broke in a thousand pieces. Owing to the scarcity of fruit and vegetables, jam becomes a necessity when camping out. More misfortunes! On unpacking we found that towels and flour, which the people at Hudson Bay Stores at Victoria had promised to put in, were missing! A real disaster!

Supper was cheering after our long day; a boiling kettle has a world of music in its hum, and to its melody we listened until it boiled. Our tea was excellent, and when one sees how easy it is to have really good tea, it is annoying to think how many people give it in an undrinkable form to their dearest friends—or otherwise—at five o'clock, who may chance to come in late, more hot water being the unfailing remedy; or else, what is quite as bad if not worse, a liquid is offered which tastes like essence of senna, because the hot water is not forthcoming.

I dozed off on my rough bed, thinking of the words of the song, "My lodging is on the cold ground." Being unaccustomed to sleep in a tent, I found myself listening to every sound; and I dreamt of grizzlies, the dreams of bears turning into the odour of fine bacon, and awoke to find it daylight, and the men preparing breakfast by the camp fire. We repacked our provisions, leaving them to be picked up on our return, and rowed back to the hotel. Three uninviting-looking towels were all the proprietor could spare. Judging by his and his sons' appearance, I should say they were a toilet article seldom used by themselves.

A bar-room, in the corner of which lay unopened cases of provisions, soon attracted our attention, and by diving into numerous boxes, we soon found flour and other things we wanted ; and having made out our own bill on a piece of cardboard, the Doctor said he would tell us what we owed on our return ; this, I may add, he did not fail to do, and of course charged exorbitantly ; but remembering Sir John Falstaff's reflection that " young men must live," we were glad to get his things at any price, as without them we should have been unable to proceed.

The Doctor's son told me his tale of woe ; how he hated the place and the life, that they had nothing but discomforts of every kind to contend with, that they used to live at Ealing where all was happiness, in a comfortable home, and of how his father had come here with the idea of making money. Not until we all became merry while unpacking their boxes of provisions did we lure a smile into his unhappy face.

The few unwary travellers, who, seeing tempting notices of the "Cowichan Hotel"—"a Paradise for Sportsmen," come from Victoria, and finding no accommodation, and nothing but discomfort, leave as soon as they can, sadder and wiser men, one night generally being more than sufficient experience of the sort of paradise it proves to be.

CHAPTER VII.

COWICHAN LAKE—OUR HAWATI INDIANS—DOWN THE RAPIDS.

> "In the valley by the river,
> In the bosom of the Forest;
> And the forest's life was in it,
> All its mystery and its magic,
> All the lightness of the birch-tree,
> All the toughness of the cedar,
> All the larch's supple sinews;
> And it floated on the river
> Like a yellow leaf in autumn."—*Longfellow.*

OUR Indians came in their dug-out canoes a long way up-stream to join us here. A slow and tedious journey, owing to the many "portages"* on the river. We were delighted, while waiting, to see them arrive; after an hour's rest they were ready to start again. Two Indians paddled in each canoe, and there was plenty of room for all our things, when the arrangements were completed. Only two of them spoke English, and of that only a few words.

* "Portages," places where the canoe has to be carried.

All of them, however, chatter Chinook, a sort of jargon originally used in trading with the Hudson's Bay Company. Most Indians on the Pacific side of the Selkirk Mountains speak this jargon (of which there are only three hundred words) as well as their own language.

Our four men were of the Hawati tribe, most excellent boatmen, but three out of the four were singularly ugly and flatfaced; "Sam," the tallest Indian, was the interpreter of the party. At the stern of Sam's canoe sat "Chuckumlilac;" unlike the others, he had the eagle nose so typical of the Red Indian; his straight black hair was cut square on his neck. They were all dressed in red shirts and blue overalls, with brightly-coloured pocket-handkerchiefs tied round their heads, this arrangement being partly to protect the head from the sun, and partly to keep their hair out of their eyes. In the other canoe were George Haltin and "Jim," the former the best hunter in the district; last fall no less than 100 deer fell to his rifle. A funny-looking little man he was, with an enormous head; he preferred going barefooted, and crept about like a snake so quietly and silently. He carried his Winchester rifle; as we paddled along I asked him which he preferred, his rifle or his squaw, and judging from the way he hugged the weapon when the question was interpreted to him, I fear the poor squaw was not in it. Jim, the last of the four Indians, sat at the stern of Algernon's canoe, and was also a good hunter.

They were very active men, and, if short of provisions, could paddle all day on little food. Exercise seemed second nature to them, but when this was over, their only idea seemed to be eating or sleeping. We amused ourselves fishing as we paddled along up the lake, and called at our old camp, for the things we had left behind in the morning; towards evening we camped in quite a charming spot, I should think twelve miles from the starting-place. Our tent was pitched on the borders of a shingle beach; close by was a running stream wending its way through alder-trees; behind us were thickly-wooded forests, and as we walked into the great woods, which stretched away miles from the shores of the lake, we were struck by the wonderful beauty of the scene. Fallen timber obstructed our way and had to be climbed over every few yards; the varieties of many-hued maples, spruce, and cedar, blending as they did with the richly-coloured mosses and lichens which hung in great festoons on every side, were to me new and strange, and the flash of some humming-birds and bright butterflies, as they flitted quickly by, disturbed by our presence, gave animation to the scene.

We enjoyed our supper of freshly-caught trout; the Indians broiled them for us, and Algernon's bread made in the frying-pan was also most successful; these things we supplemented with bacon, baked potatoes, some fresh butter (brought from Victoria) and a plentiful supply of tea, which one drinks at all times here without any bad effects. Hunger is after all the best sauce, and cooking to us being a novelty, we were much pleased with our small feats in that line.

The shingle beach made rather a hard bed! gravel and pebbles cannot be like a spring-mattress, consequently my bones ached for a little time after getting up, but it was dry, which our beds of the previous night certainly were not. Sleeping in the open air is very different from repose in a comfortable bed in a house, but has this advantage that one always awakes cheerful and refreshed; and even the sluggard, were he here, would not care to linger with daylight and sunshine round him everywhere. Algernon and his hunter departed early with their rifles, and not long after returned with a deer. The Indian's mode of carrying it was strange; after skinning the animal, he put all the good meat and haunches into the skin, of which he made a sack, and thus carried it back to camp.

With two of the Indians, I went fishing; here the fly seemed useless. First of all I tried a large, then a small one, and after that a Scotch burn trout fly, but all with no success. In the middle of the lake we saw two Indians fishing, and feeling instinctively that they would know best what to use in their own water, I signed to our men to join them, and we found at the bottom of their canoe about twenty-four beautiful trout and charr (*Salmo salvelinus*), varying in size from about two to six pounds each. The owners of the boat were a man and his squaw, who lived at the foot of the lake. The squaw showed me their spoils with evident pleasure. After looking at me as if I were a curiosity from the British Museum, she devoted her attention to our flies, which she regarded most contemptuously. They then showed us a spoon with which they were trolling, and baited us a hook with a piece of silvery-looking trout.

Our luck from this time began to change, and we soon had a plentiful supply of beautiful fish for our supper, and some of these, I have every reason to believe, were charr, for they were singularly rich in colour, seven rows of gold and yellow spots on either side, the back similar in tint to a mackerel, the under part being silvery white, with a beautiful pink stripe down both sides, the lower fins bright scarlet, the head small, the tail and back fins mottled like tortoise-shell, and the flesh of a rich coral colour.*

Trolling is not the same pleasure as fly-fishing; there is no skill required in drawing in hand over hand on a strong line a three or six pound trout; but we, being hungry, were glad to get them. For when neither butcher nor fishmonger are near, the question of how to fill the pot becomes a most interesting one.

The Indians were of course delighted with the venison, and to-night's supper of venison steaks and broiled trout was a pleasant change. The Indians generally cook their meat and fish in the way I have already described, on sticks before the fire. These Indians also fried venison steaks in oil, adding Worcester sauce after taking them

* The two species of trout—yellow trout (*Sa'mo fario*) and the great lake trout (*Salmo ferox*)—can always be distinguished from charrs by the characteristic of having two complete rows of teeth in the vomer or central bone in the roof of the mouth, whilst in charrs the vomer has only a few teeth, and those in the most forward part.—*H. Cholmondeley Pennell.*

off the fire, the result being equal to any chef's method. How they eat! One Indian can consume more meat than four white men, often 10 or 12 lbs. at a sitting! The Hudson Bay allowance of pemmican for an Indian boy used to be 6 lbs. per day.

We saw a richly-coloured snake gliding about among the stones while we were waiting for supper, but he got into a hole before we could kill him.

July 14th.—An early start. Breakfasted 5 A.M. To-day caught twenty-seven trout, the largest 6 lbs.

The lake scenery was very beautiful, reminding me of Scotland; but the mountain sides here are more densely wooded, being covered with enormous timber.

We camped at the head of the lake under huge cedar-trees, the most beautiful camping-ground imaginable. Much fallen timber and drift-wood lay about here; the latter proved useful for the camp fires.

The timber by which we were surrounded would be of immense value if in an accessible place; but the fallen trees lie here until they become covered with masses of ferns and lichens. These mosses and lichens are of the richest colours and rarest beauty.

Some day doubtless saw-mills, railways, and steamboats will change this lovely scene, but fortunately for the present, nature remains undisturbed.

Our Indians sleep in the open air, and have their own camp fire, round which they talk in low musical voices for hours, while they whittle out new paddles for their canoes.

July 18*th*.—Four days have passed in this delightful paradise; regretfully we must leave it. A glorious haze hung over everything in the sunlight of early morning; by 6 A.M. the canoes were packed, and we quitted this lovely retreat. The heat was overpowering as the hours wore on, and though it was a day of days for painting, the reflections in the water being so wonderfully clear and beautiful, still lying back in the canoe and doing nothing seemed pleasanter, while the ceaseless stroke of the paddles, and the varied and melancholy cries of the loons (the great northern diver), of which there were many in this lake, were the only sounds which broke the stillness.

In this way we paddled along; and when we landed, more than half way down the lake, it was afternoon. Our Indians gathered berries—we found wild raspberries on bushes 12 to 16 feet high. Resting in the shade was pleasant, and having arranged my blanket on a mossy bank under my weary head, I fell asleep, and at length awoke to find our Indians ready to start again, so we all took our places, and off we went.

They paddled and we killed time by trolling as we went along; part of the time I fished with a spoon on a trout rod, and landed a 4-lb. trout after excellent play, which amusement the Indians failed to appreciate, their only idea being to kill. We camped when it was getting dark. Our Indians were very sulky, and we had to do everything for ourselves. They are often difficult to deal with, taking offence for no apparent reason; the only thing to be done was to leave them alone to recover their tempers.

An early start arranged for to-morrow.

I bathed in the lake most days while the men were preparing breakfast, it was so refreshing, and the water not in the least cold, and one day heard a whirr over my head, but could not see anything for a moment, and then descried two tiny humming-birds hovering above me. They looked like large bright-coloured butterflies at a little distance.

One of the Indians brought us a huge dragon-fly, but just as we were about to transfix him with a pin he fortunately for himself took flight.

July 19*th.*—Indifferent fishing as we paddled along to-day. We called at a raft on which, in a wooden "shack," * lived a young Englishman named Maitland, where we left a fine trout in return for one he had given us on our way up. He, like many others, had bought a block of land, and was waiting for times to improve, a common way of trying to make money out here.

We stopped at the foot of the lake, at the hotel, which looked as uninviting as ever, and again saw the melancholy son of the house, and gave him a 6-lb. trout in hope of cheering him; and having paid our bill for provisions, we said good-bye to the Cowichan Lake and entered the river. Our Indians had another fit of the sulks when Algernon refused to treat them to whisky at the hotel bar, as we were now going to run a series of rapids.

* Rough board hut.

One of the laws of the country most strictly enforced is that against giving Indians spirits in any form, and the fine for the infraction is $50. In spite of this law, people do give it them occasionally, and Indians have been known themselves to inform against the man who has stood treat. Spirits almost always affect them in the same way; for the time they become perfectly mad, and moderation is unknown among them. After our return we heard that "Chuckumlilac," the Indian who sat in the bow of my canoe, had killed his brother with a blow from his paddle after one of these drinking-revels; so we felt thankful we had not encouraged them at a time when all their powers of quickness and daring were absolutely necessary for our safety.

On we went, faster and faster. One moment the Indian in the bow used his paddle, the next he seized his pole, and, with the most marvellous quickness and dexterity, eluded many dangers from rocks and logs which, had we touched them at the pace the canoe was going, would have upset us all into the tumultuous stream. By inserting his pole in the bank or on some projecting point of rock, the canoe was made to swing round, and in this way we avoided many obstructions which threatened our frail craft.

The delights of the journey—how can one recall them all? The flowing river was a bright green colour, and, though very deep, we could see stones lying at the bottom of some of the quiet pools, and occasionally some frightened trout darted away as the canoe passed. When we came to white foam and rough water, we knew we were nearing a rapid, and I sat very still, wondering how we should pass through. The little lithe Indian seated in the bow, Chuckumlilac, chose his course at a glance. I shall always see him as he appeared to-day; his brown, walnut-coloured skin, his black hair, cut squarely round his neck, his thin wrinkled face, and his sharp eagle eyes; round his head was tied a coloured handkerchief, and the rest of his dress was in harmonious tints of blue and red; in his belt hung a large knife. With what grace and ease he moved!

Sam, the other Indian, who paddled in the stern of the canoe, we could not induce to be cheerful; he did not like the white men. Several times he had complained that they had been hard to the Indians, and doubtless he had cause for doing so. As the country gets settled up, the Indians are losing their hunting-grounds, and the more discerning of their race see that they are being crowded out by the white man, though the Indians both round Victoria and the coast are such good workers that they are still pretty well holding their own. There is a pride and dignity in the people one cannot help admiring. We heard both of their dirt and dishonesty, but had to complain of neither. Several times when I dropped or mislaid things in camp, they were returned to me, and the men took the greatest trouble in searching for anything that had been lost.

To return to my Indians. The two canoes kept together whilst running down the river, Algernon's leading the way. The ease with which the Indians steered through the rapids was wonderful. Rocky channels, narrow enough already, were often made still narrower by fallen timber, in many cases this left only room for the canoe to pass; in others the axe had to be used to clear a way. When there was a sharp bend in the river, and not room to swing the canoe with the paddle or pole, the Indian in the stern jumped out on to a log or rock, and with a line from the stern swung her into the best channel, and jumped in just as she fled down the rapid.

The risks of a trip on a river full of rapids are considerable. One mistake in a bad place with pole or paddle either upsets or smashes the canoe, and then the chances are against a safe landing. When we reached the first falls which were too high to run in the canoes, we jumped out into the shoal water, and wading from rock to rock with our "kit," got to the bank, and there clambered along as best we could to the foot of the falls. The canoes were half-carried, half-floated to a point from which they could be lowered by ropes over the fall, which done, our canoe was then reloaded, and we were off again.

I was glad that my tweed petticoat reached only to my knees, and with long boots, a flannel shirt, and Norfolk jacket, I could jump from rock to rock in a way that surprised even myself. All the men were occupied with the baggage and canoes, so it was fortunate I could get about without help. Only twice, when the portages were through rather deep water, Algernon carried me over.

In Canada and New Brunswick, where Algernon has

CHARMS OF OPEN-AIR LIFE.

principally hunted, the canoes used were generally birch-bark; here they are all dug-outs, generally of cedar; they are made on a beautiful model for the work they have to do, and are very light, the wood being only half an inch in thickness.

Sometimes, as we got into heavy rapids, it seemed impossible that they would allow themselves to be guided, but as we glided through the water at about ten miles an hour, sometimes rushing past a large rock, at others within a few inches of a sweeper, as they call the trees which hang across the river just clear of the water, we saw how skilfully the Indians steered, and felt when each danger was passed the same sort of excitement as when clearing a big fence with hounds. The banks of the river were lovely, green with maidenhair ferns and mosses, whilst high on both sides towered big trees.

The day's work being over, we camped on a bank, and amused ourselves fishing for an hour or two before supper, and were able with the fly to catch a few nice trout; and after a good supper were lulled to sleep by the murmur of running waters.

Wonderful is the rest to body and mind in this kind of wild life. I marvel no more that weary and disappointed men go into the woods to find oblivion.

"No tears,
Dim the sweet look which Nature wears."

There is often solace in the sight of God's grand and glorious works, and care is dwarfed, for human plans appear insignificant indeed, compared with the great designs of creation.

The camp was roused at 3.30 A.M., and after a hasty meal of biscuits and tea, we paddled down the remainder of the Cowichan River; heavy dew and mist hung over everything when we started, but after an hour or two the day cleared and was bright. One of the Indians shot a deer from the canoe, but we could not find it in the " chapperal." *

We shot a good many rapids this morning, but none so rough as those higher up the river. On reaching Duncan, we were greeted by several squaws, who seemed to have much news to tell our boatmen. We ourselves were glad to hurry off to the nice little inn, which goes by the name of the Guamachen Hotel, where we enjoyed breakfast which we had not been obliged to cook for ourselves.

We then called on Duncan and his wife—nice Scotch people who were the first settlers here, and after whom the village takes its name. They have a farm and orchard, and seemed getting on well. With his assistance we settled up with the Indians, and left for Victoria by the only train which passes this place daily from Nanaimo.

It is very difficult to keep one's clothes tidy in camp, as perpetually the fire "wants fixing up," or the kettle boils over, or perhaps one sees the frying-pan sliding quietly into the fire; then, clean or dirty, one must go to the rescue. I found the best way to avoid having to wash my hands perpetually was to wear a long pair of dogskin gloves, and to keep them on most of the day.

* The bush.

CHAPTER VIII.

VICTORIA—PORTLAND—NOTES ABOUT ALASKA.

"The brotherhood not of equality, nor of likeness, but of giving and receiving; the souls that are unlike, and the nations that are unlike, each receiving something from and of the others' glory."—*Ruskin*.

Victoria, August 20th.—Played tennis in Sir Matthew Begbie's garden. He was absent, but we went there with the clergyman's daughters. The iron church of which their father is rector was erected by Lady Burdett Coutts.

There was great excitement about an Indian rising on the Skena river. The battery of artillery quartered at Victoria left for the Skena the day before we arrived. All the trouble was caused by stupid interference on the the part of the police. An Indian dispute had been settled by the offender being shot—justly according to their views. The police tried to arrest the chief who had done this, and, failing to do so, shot him dead. All the neighbouring Indians rose, and the few white men were surrounded in a fort near Hazelton. In Vancouver Island the Indians have not received the same fair treatment as in the North-West Territory; reserves have been taken from them, and others they do not like substituted; this they deeply resent.

We found it would cost us $60 each to make a journey to San Francisco. We thought and spoke of taking another trip to the north end of this island, to a place called Comox, but the curator of the museum, a good sportsman, told Algernon it was too early in the season to kill mountain goats; so we decided to go to San Francisco *viâ* Tacoma, and took berths on the steamer which sails on Monday.

We visited the Chinese quarters of the city, which we found very interesting; there were many excellent shops where oriental goods of all sorts were sold. We found the Chinese extremely civil and obliging. I bought a pair of large earthenware dragons, which we sent home round Cape Horn, in one of the Hudson's Bay Company's steamers.

Afterwards we spent a quarter of an hour in a Chinese druggist's shop—all the medicines were dispensed in a dry state, and we were told were infused by the buyers according to the prescription which the chemist wrote outside each packet.

A duty of $50 is imposed on all Chinamen landing in this country; this appears hard, as they do most of the labour here. In the old days some people tried importing servants from England, but this did not answer, they generally married directly, and we were told of an amusing instance. A gentleman had engaged three maid-servants, but the vessel in which they sailed from England stopped at San Francisco *en route;* they all married there, whilst the unfortunate man who had hoped to have the comfort of English servants, had their journeys to pay for, though he never even saw them.

The opening of the Canadian Pacific Railway has made Vancouver Island much more accessible. Many people here remember when it took six weeks to reach it from England, now the journey can be accomplished in fourteen days.

After dining with friends, we rowed up an inlet at the entrance to a river inside the harbour called "the gorge," which looks like an ornamental lake. There were many pleasure-boats filled with happy-looking people enjoying the lovely evening, and in the harbour we saw steamers preparing to sail for all parts of the world, and I almost wished we were going in one of them to the Sandwich Islands, to China or Japan.

The Princess Louise and the Marquis of Lorne were at Victoria for three months when he was Governor-General of Canada, and they were most popular with all classes. An amusing anecdote is told about the Princess. Soon after her arrival she went into a shop and bought a small toy. Having forgotten her purse, she said, "Will you trust me?" The man looked at her, and said, "Yes; I guess you are good for half a dollar." On finding out afterwards that it was the Princess to whom he had spoken in this way, he was so mortified he said he would have given everything in his "store" not to have done it.

After a busy evening, packing, by 11 P.M. we were on

the Tacoma boat, on our way to San Francisco. The steamer did not leave the harbour until 4 A.M., so we had a good sleep on board; but when she began to move the vibration was very great. The old story—powerful engines and a very light hull.

We had a capital cabin, with a private door opening to the deck. The ship was built like an American riverboat, with two tiers of cabins and old-fashioned beam-engines; food vile, though plentiful. The route was down the Puget Sound. The scenery was rather disappointing, the only fine sight being Mount Ranier, or Tacoma, as it is now called, forty miles off and 14,600 feet high, a solitary snow-covered peak, rising into the blue sky. We called at Port Townshend, and afterwards at Seattle. The steamer remained here three hours, and we amused ourselves by walking through the town—a very primitive place, only two or three streets being finished, the rest of the blocks unoccupied.*

More money is made and lost in Canada and the States by gambling in town lots in new cities than in almost any other way. This place seems no exception, and we were told that there was a "*boom*" on here, which means that the prices of land were rising to some absurdly high figure.

On our arrival at Tacoma we found quite a large town, where four years ago stood a pine forest. They have called their city after the mountain. The steamers start from this place for Alaska; the Oregon and Californian

* Since we returned home the place has been destroyed by fire.

Railway runs also from here in connection with the Northern Pacific Railway. The hotel is finely situated, standing on a high cliff overlooking the valley and mountain beyond; at high tide the sea covers the low ground, making it look like an immense lake; for weeks at a time the mountain is invisible, being enveloped in clouds, but we were fortunate in seeing it.

We observed during dinner something which appeared to us unusual. Two small children (Americans), a girl and boy, the latter certainly not more than five years old, and the girl perhaps a little older, came in at 8.30, sat down at a table near us, and ordered their dinner, even looking over the "*wine carte*" which was handed to them. Fortunately they drank milk, but they ate a most unwholesome dinner, of which lobster and large ice creams were two of the component parts. The menu card must have puzzled them as one of the dishes was "*Tête de veau en torture.*" I thought more likely it would be the little boy who would thus suffer. When they finished we asked the small person if he had enjoyed his dinner; he crossed his arms behind his back, surveyed us leisurely, and merely said, "You bet."

A large cinnamon bear belongs to the hotel; he seems well looked after, and appears good-tempered, and devoted to his keeper. We were amused to see this huge creature playing with a broom as if he were a kitten.

July 25th.—We left Tacoma for San Francisco. We had some difficulty in getting to the station, owing to the want of carriages, and had to drive with some odious people who took the best places, and were both rude and disagreeable.

The journey to Portland was not very interesting; the Columbia river is crossed near here by a large steam ferry, which takes two trains over at a time. It is a very fine river, and all Canadians say here should have been the boundary of Canada, as it forms a natural frontier; but the boundaries were settled chiefly in England, where great ignorance then existed as to the geography of the country, and the Viceroy of that time seems to have been equally mistaken in allowing such a boundary as the present one to have been decided on. The story goes that some adviser of the Viceroy's, more sportsman than patriot, said, "Let the Columbia go. What is the good of a river where the salmon won't take a fly." During the run of fish, many thousand salmon are canned daily.*

Some of the small islands off the coast of Vancouver are half American and half Canadian. Portland itself is on the Williamette river, and from Robinson's Hill, which is in the upper part of the town, we had a magnificent view of the Columbia and Williamette rivers, and of the Great Cascade range with all its glittering peaks, and on the

* " Until the last three years the canning industry of the Columbia showed a steady increase; in 1883 the total pack was not less than 629,400 cases, valued at $3,147,000: each of the last four seasons has, however, shown a marked falling off, the entire export since 1866, exclusive of the salt pack in barrels and of the large local consumption, amounts to 371,116,000 lbs., or about 25,000,000 fish."

extreme right, 78 miles distant, the snowy crown of Mount Jefferson. Across the river, 50 miles off, rose Mount Hood, one of the most beautiful mountains on the coast; to the north-east stood out the crests of Mount Adams and Mount St. Helen's, and in the same direction on a very clear day might be descried the great Tacoma, the monarch of the range; all these five peaks were white with snow.

We had a series of mishaps on reaching Portland; tired of the bad food on the cars, we decided to wait until we arrived there. We were desperately hungry, and on inquiring for the Oregon and California Railway Station and a restaurant, were told by a crowd of greedy cabmen "both a long way off." Hiring a carriage, we were driven 50 yards to the restaurant. There we found an excellent menu and wretched food. Starting again, our driver took us a couple of hundred yards, and again stopped, this time to convey us over the ferry; his charge so far was $2, and he wanted another to cross the ferry; but having been sufficiently swindled, we removed our baggage, and dismissed him, the station being on the other side. Thus sometimes fares the globe-trotter!

Money is certainly the god worshipped "out West." It was constantly the topic of conversation among our fellow-travellers, until we were weary of hearing about these "corner lots" and "booming cities;" the pursuit of wealth is not so apparent in England, though many are hasting to be rich in our country also. Here it seemed to me so many had no time for anything else. The haste and unrest, whether in making a fortune, taking a journey, or

even eating food, surprised me, and I could not help often
saying to myself, why all this needless hurry ? Happily

> "There are in this loud stunning tide
> Of human care and crime,
> With whom the melodies abide
> Of the everlasting chime;
> Who carry music in their heart
> Through dusty lane and wrangling mart,
> Plying their daily task with busier feet,
> Because their secret souls a holy strain repeat;"

and if this were not so to counteract the materialism of
the world, how would it be?

July 26th.—Travelling in heated cars made me wish we
were still camping out in the cool green woods. We
passed Mount Shasta, 14,440 feet high, and after leaving
the volcanic regions of gloomy-looking rocks which lie for
many miles round it, we found ourselves running down
countless zigzags in the mountains, with uncomfortably
short turns at the corners, and diving still further down
the valley we arrived in the Cañon of the Sacramento.
Following the river brought us at last into the fertile
country of the Sacramento valley, where prosperous farms,
heavily-laden orchards, corn-fields ripe with golden grain,
and bronzed peasants, made a happy and abundant landscape. There was an air about these people which
reminded me of Spain, the picturesque grouping and
colours which Phillips painted so well; no doubt many
of them could tell of Spanish ancestry, and many of them
still have Spanish names.

The "Buffet" arrangements on this railway were very inferior to the Canadian Pacific Railway. This is a matter of consideration when one travels three days in succession. At some of the places where we stopped to dine, the food was uneatable, the tables nearly covered with small dishes containing many things, but nothing good, and the masses of black flies everywhere were not appetising. After all, there are many worse things than the slices of beef or mutton with which we so often find fault in our refreshment-rooms at home.

The train ran over a skunk in the night. I was awakened in my berth by a stifling sensation, as were all the other passengers, and it was quite twenty minutes before the terrible odour died away.

We travelled with some pleasant Americans, who were returning from a visit to Alaska. They told us of the delights of a journey there, and from what they said, we regretted that we were unable to go; they said that with the exception of two places in the Sound, they were in calm water the whole time.

A trip to Alaska takes nearly three weeks; and from Victoria to Sitka and back again, with everything supplied except wine, the fare is $95 each.

It is pleasant to hear impressions about new places from people who have visited them; the guide-books are so inaccurate, that very little reliance can be placed on their descriptions.

The principal sights of Alaska are Mount St. Elias, the highest mountain in North America (19,000 feet high);

as yet no party has succeeded in reaching the summit, although several attempts have been made. We heard that the whole distance from base to summit has to be climbed on ice and snow; the "Muir" glacier, the largest in the world, is also seen there, the toe of which measures more than one mile across.

The State of Alaska was purchased by the United States Government from Russia in 1867, for $7,200,000; the value of the seal fishery alone pays the Government 4½ per cent. on the outlay. It is a pity it is not English territory, as it lies across the northern boundary of Canada, and abounds in rich mines. "Alaska" is a corruption of Al-ay-ek-sa, the name given by the natives to the mainland, signifying great country. It contains nearly 600,000 square miles of territory; Sitka, the old capital of the Russian possessions in America, was the religious, commercial, political and educational centre; with the change of government, came a new people into the country, and the majority of Russians left, their places being taken by Americans.

At Sitka, there is a fine Greek church with silver gates, built by the Russians.

The white settlers have not set the example they ought to have done to the Indians, hence the saying which has passed into a proverb at Sitka, "It takes twenty years to make an Indian into a Boston man, but only six months to make a Boston man into an Indian."

White men buy the Indian girls from their mothers at ages varying from ten to twenty years, for from $50 to

§75. The Indian women believe themselves honourably married, and make good wives, but, alas! the men do not hold the same views, and often leave them.

The population consists of 17,617 Esquimaux; 2,145 Aleuts; 1,756 Creoles; 5,000 Tinnehs; 6,437 Thleigets; 788 Hydahs, and 500 whites; making a total of 38,843.

The Metlahkatlah, known as Duncan's mission, is one of the most successful in the far north. For reasons which take too long to explain here, but are nevertheless much to be regretted, Mr. Duncan removed into United States territory from British Columbia, taking with him 1,000 Indians, about the most civilised and the finest of their race on British soil.

CHAPTER IX.

SAN FRANCISCO AND CHINA-TOWN.—THE CHINESE
QUESTION.

"The strongest recollections seem to be,
Like latent music, in the commonest things;
We put our hand upon them passing by,
And rudely touch the unsuspected strings."
Clifford Harrison.

Occidental Hotel, San Francisco, July 28th.—We came here late last night, preferring this to the "Palace Hotel," where one is known only by a number! Many people go there only to say that they have stayed in the largest hotel in the world.

This morning, after breakfast, we mounted one of the Cable Cars at the corner of the street near this hotel, and went a distance of four miles, going up steep ascents most part of the way, until the gardens of the Golden Gate Park were reached; there we changed into a train, which was furnished with open cars; it took us over a sandy-looking desert to the Cliff House, one of the sights of San Francisco.

CLIFF HOUSE.

The Cable Cars amused me, this being the first time I had seen them; it looked quite startling to feel them moving along without steam or horses, propelled by an underground cable, and they go either up or down hill with equal ease. Carriages are seldom seen in San Francisco, owing to the number of street cars that always block the principal thoroughfares, and people living in the country who have carriages, rarely bring them into the town.

When we got near the Cliff House we had some wonderful views of the blue sea, and the great waves breaking all along the coast were beautiful and grand; and yet there are many persons "Out West" who have never seen the sea. I met a woman of fifty on our journey from Victoria, B.C., who told me she had never seen either the sea or a mountain until a few weeks before, having spent all her life on the prairie. "But," she added, "my man has now made his pile, and we are having a look around." I asked her which impressed her most. She said simply, "Oh, the ocean! the longer I gaze the more I love it, until I feel I can never leave it."

We soon came in sight of the three large rocks, where the sea-lions have their home, and we looked at them for some time through telescopes and glasses; the rocks on which they live are about half a mile from the shore. No one is allowed to molest them; there are supposed to be about 500 of them, some are enormous, measuring 16 to 18 feet in length, and they are very savage if disturbed. Some of the old males are much scarred from fighting, and it was curious to observe their slow and awkward movements, as they pulled themselves up and off the slippery rocks. On the Sutro heights, above the Cliff House, are charming gardens, laid out by Mr. Sutro; they are open to the public, and show what can be done by irrigation on this sandy soil; for there the desert is transformed as if by magic, and all kinds of beautiful flowers grow in the greatest luxuriance. I asked one of the gardeners, a German, the name of a plant which much pleased me; there were beds of it with flowers of all colours, growing creeper-like on the ground, the bloom somewhat resembling a wild rose. The gardener gave me a large parcel of cuttings, they were portulaccas; he also gave me cuttings of *Mesembryanthemum cordifolium*, which are pretty for edging beds. I packed and sent them to my gardener in England, but they did not carry. Both these plants can be grown from seed, and thrive well in this country.

The climate here is perfect: in winter no colder than at this time of year; indeed, residents consider the month of August the coldest in San Francisco, because of the trade-winds, which, however, did not annoy us, though they generally blew from two to six o'clock in the afternoon. We heard by our English letters much about the cold and wet summer at home, but with us it has been perpetual sunshine, two wet days at Quebec and one on the prairie being our record for three months.

An American lady, speaking about Matthew Arnold's article on 'Civilization in America,' remarked that, though severe, it was on the whole true, except when he said that all children read Roe's novels instead of those of Sir Walter Scott. "There he is wrong," she remarked. "In the East they had hardly heard of G. P. Roe; on this side he was certainly better known." She also added, "If Matthew Arnold thought so little of our civilization, why did he not show us a better example? He did not even wear evening clothes at the largest parties he attended in America, which rather annoyed people. As a writer he is admired, but his article was very hard on us as a nation."

The impression a stranger receives is that Carlyle and Emerson are adored, especially the latter, and that Ingersoll holds no place among the learned. His articles have been refuted by several, and most ably answered in a small book, which has reached its eighth edition, and is entitled, 'Notes on Ingersoll,' by the Rev. L. A. Lambart, a Catholic priest.

We wandered all through China-Town. Several guides offered to take charge of us, but we preferred seeing what we could by ourselves. If it were not for the ordinary style of building the houses, we could fancy ourselves in Pekin or Canton. There is a population of over 40,000 Chinese in San Francisco. They all live in the quarter called "China-Town," apart from every one else, pursuing mostly their own work and trades. We saw Chinese hurrying in every direction, for the Celestial is always busy, and therefore in haste. We passed many stores containing goods of all kinds, and by looking through the doorway we saw how the people were employed. In one shop there were bootmakers at work; in another sewing machines were busy. The Chinese excel in all kinds of labour, and are so frugal that they can undersell the Americans even in cheap tailoring. But here the sweating system is also in vogue, and it is the middleman who is making a profit. A pair of blue overalls (an article of clothing worn by almost every workman) is made by the men employed in these tailors' shops for a quarter-dollar, or one shilling of our money. We passed many provision-shops, and very unpalatable the food looked; thin pieces of meat, dried ducks, bundles of sausages, and stale pork being the principal things we noticed. There were baskets of vegetables of all kinds in front of the windows of these shops, and these seemed to find a ready sale.

Then, through a narrow door far under the level of an ordinary cellar, we saw the barber at work in his shop. The front part of a Chinaman's head is kept shaved; the back is arranged into a pigtail. Where nature has not been bountiful, and I doubt if she is ever sufficiently so— it makes no difference, as all appear to have black silk plaited in with their hair to make the pigtail longer; it usually reaches down the back as far as the knees. In China it is thought disrespectful to roll it round one's head, but in this country the Chinese servants do it in order to get the pigtails out of the way. When the Chinaman's forehead is shaved and his pigtail arranged, he is by no means out of the hands of the barber, for the inside of his ears have also to be shaved. We saw this being done, and rather a disagreeable process it seemed; but I suppose the Celestial must suffer with the rest of the world *pour être beau*.

We found all the Chinese civil and obliging. Before entering their Joss-houses, as they call their places of worship, their shops, or restaurants, we asked permission to do so, which was readily granted. Among the anti-Chinese party the custom is to treat the Celestials as rudely as possible. We did not wish to do this, nor did the Americans who accompanied us. We went into the shop of a goldsmith, who was beating out gold rings, and we saw some that he had finished. He was working by a small reed lamp, similar to those found in the ruins of Pompeii, and by him also stood a very curious old pair of scales, with which he weighed his rings before selling them by weight. Though we did not buy, as we passed out he raised his head from his work and nodded to us.

Our next visit was to a restaurant, and having bowed to the man in charge, we passed in. Saw two cooks making little rolls; which, when finished, were stamped with a Chinese mark. These rolls are filled with mincemeat, and are sent to Chinamen all over Canada and America. We did not like the taste of them; and, after seeing them passed into the ovens, we went upstairs. In Chinese restaurants here, the higher up you go the more you pay, and for this reason, the houses not being built on the lines of a Chinaman's ideal, it is only on the upper floor that seats n, and a garden on the roof with verandahs to sit

I

in, can be obtained. On the first floor we saw an eating-house for the poorer class of workmen; each table being partitioned off from the next with screens. After mounting to the upper-floor, we found ourselves in a charming Chinese house; all the fittings and furniture were of home workmanship, the chairs and tables being of ebony, beautifully inlaid with mother-of-pearl, while valuable carvings, screens, and lamps were tastefully arranged. Both the Chinese and ᴄhinese have certainly perfect taste. Six or eight round tables were neatly laid out for dinner. The dishes were so small, that though there were many of them piled up with fruits, tiny pieces of fish, and other things, it looked to me like a doll's dinner-party, and not a repast prepared for hungry men. Opposite to each guest were tiny plates, a china spoon, a pair of ivory chopsticks, and a small glass bowl, containing some kind of liqueur.

We passed through the kitchen, where several cooks were busily engaged with their tiny pans; but a hungry navvy would have eaten up everything we saw in a very short time. Can this be all the food Celestials need? Is the bird's-nest soup so very sustaining, or do they not eat in the quantities Europeans do? The last question is answered negatively, the problem solved; Chinamen can live on rice, and nothing else, doing the hardest work in mines, or manual labour all the time; and this is how they can save so much where other men must eat to live.

We were attracted by the sounds of merry voices, and passed on, and soon were intently watching a dinner-party from behind a screen. Ten Chinamen were dining together; by their dress we concluded they were well-to-do merchants—some of whom are very wealthy—they were evidently enjoying excellent jokes; as we watched them from our undignified position, we observed that in this, as well as in some of the other private rooms, was an alcove, with the opium pipe; by it, on a luxurious couch, one of the guests was lying in a sort of stupor, apparently unconscious; the other guests seemed to take no notice of him, as if there was nothing unusual in his condition.

We passed into another room, and had tea; it was nicely served in beautiful oriental china cups. In front of each person stood a covered cup on a little stand: and the tea-leaves were placed in each of these; a Chinaman came in and poured boiling water from a bronze kettle over the leaves, the cover was replaced, and in a few minutes the tea was ready; and, with care, was poured into another cup, and the one containing the leaves acted as a kind of tea-pot, and was refilled with boiling water. Excellent tea it was, but somewhat costly; so much so, that our American friends, who bought 1 lb., had $5 to pay for it. Green tea is preferred, the flavour is more flowery and delicate, when infused being of a pale colour. Our tea was served with plates of cakes, nuts, and ginger. During the time we were having it a band played in the verandah, and such a band! The noise made by the five musicians was deafening; but as three of their number had gongs (or something very like them), and the fourth a drum, it was not surprising. The fifth musician had a sort of trumpet, and when the gongs at intervals ceased playing, the trumpet, single-handed, produced most discordant tones, mingled with wails, which were meant for singing. We were thankful when this performance ceased, though, judging by the acclamations of the rest of the audience, the music was considered excellent.

We visited several joss-houses, and were saddened by the rows of idols we saw, some of which were very hideous. The Chinese do not pray to the good spirits, we were told, as they do them no harm, but to the evil ones. All these poor souls seem to be in a state of the greatest spiritual darkness, having few redeeming points in their religion. There is no devoutness in their joss-houses, the men who are in charge sleep about the doors; those who come in to say their prayers write them, and afterwards burn them in an oven.

Looking in at several of the opium dens, we saw as much of them as we wished; we heard enough about the horrors of this vice, and occasionally we passed a Chinaman who looked like a ghost—an unmistakable victim.

Some of the people we met could not reason, nor even speak quietly on the subject of the Chinese question. The moment anything was said about China or the Chinese, they talked without weighing either their words or their arguments. With such a person it was our fate to travel in the cars for three days, coming from Portland. Unsought, he joined in our conversation, which happened to be on the subject of the Chinese; he remarked, "The Chinese are of no use in San Francisco, or, for that matter, in America, and they must go, for they are parasites; dirty, useless, lying, and dishonest." With some difficulty I was able to remark that at Victoria the English people told me they were most valuable as domestic servants, where no other servants were available, and did a great deal of work; he continued his abuse. "They were the curse of his country, and brought over disease and many other dreadful things." I asked him if he had ever been to China-Town. He confessed that, though he had lived in the city of San Francisco twenty years, he had never been there, nor had he ever allowed his wife to go, nor to have any dealings with the Chinese. He then advised Algernon not to allow me to visit China-Town, as it would be at the peril of our lives from small-pox, lepros, and other horrors.

The subject lapsed, as we did not trouble to talk much more to him, though for two days we travelled onwards in the same dusty and hot cars.

I do not know why it is, but when nearing one's destination, ideas are often exchanged, and he again joined us; but I think he must have forgotten our conversation of the previous day, for to our amusement he began telling us of the best shops in San Francisco, adding, "When my wife wants Chinese bargains, she buys them of a smuggler who calls once a week at our house; our home is full of valuable things we have got from him at cheap prices."

Fancy taking advice from such a creature!

Of course we went to China-Town, and profited by our visit; how often while travelling one comes across these extraordinary types of humanity, who are contradictions in themselves.

Before ending my remarks about the Chinese, I would quote extracts which appeared in the columns of the Vienna press. The Chinese question is important enough to deserve dispassionate handling, and to call for the highest degree of statesmanship in dealing with it. The extracts are the writing of so great an authority as Baron Alexander Von Hübner, formerly the Austrian Ambassador to France, who for years past has been travelling round the world, and who is the author of many learned works. He says :—

"Whoever speaks of the important changes on the face
" of the globe must not allow China to pass unremarked.
" The war of England and France against the Celestial
" Empire was an historical fact of world-wide importance,
" not because of the military successes achieved, the most
" famous of which was the plunder and destruction of the
" Imperial Palace at Pekin, but because the allies cast down
" the walls through which 400,000,000 of inhabitants were
" hermetically closed in from the outer world. With the
" intention of opening China to Europeans, the globe has
" been thrown open to the Chinese. Who travels now
" through the flowery kingdom ? No one with the exception
" of the missionaries whose presence was already tolerated
" there, and in addition to these, there were a few explorers.
" But the Chinese are streaming over the greater part of the

" globe, and are also forming colonies, albeit after their own
" fashion. Highly gifted, although inferior to the Caucasian
" in the highest spheres of mental activity, endowed with
" an untiring industry though temperate to the utmost
" abstemiousness, frugal, a born merchant of probity ever
" true to his word, a first-class cultivator especially in
" gardening, distinguished in every kind of handicraft, the
" son of the middle kingdom, slowly, surely, and unre-
" marked, is supplanting the Europeans wherever they are
" brought together. I am speaking of them only as I have
" found them. In 1871, the entire English trade with
" China, amounting then as now to £42,000,000 sterling,
" was transacted by English firms. The four great houses,
" one of which was American, were in Shanghai, while the
" smaller ones were distributed among the treaty ports.
" Added to these were the middle-men, as the sale of
" English imports in the interior of the Empire was effected
" by English merchants. In addition to this, the firm of
" Russell & Co. owned twenty steamers, that kept up the
" commercial intercourse between the treaty ports extend-
" ing to the Yangtse river. Now-a-days, with the exception
" of some great influential English firms, all the same trade,
" together with the Russell steamers, has passed into the
" hands of Chinese merchants or of Chinese corporations.
" In Macao, for 400 years in possession of the Portuguese,
" are to be seen magnificent palaces, some of which date
" from the sixteenth century; they are situated in the
" finest part of the city, where the Chinese are not in the
" habit of building, and yet the greater part of these palaces

"have passed by purchase into the hands of rich Chinese,
" and are inhabited by them. On my first visit to
" Singapore in 1871, the population consisted of 100 white
" families, of 20,000 Malays, and a few thousand Chinese.
" On my return there the beginning of 1884, the population
" was divided according to the official census into 100 white
" families, 20,000 Malays, and 86,000 Chinese. A new
" Chinese town had sprung up, with magnificent stores,
" beautiful residences and pagodas. I imagined I was
" transported to Canton. The country lying to the south
" of Anglo-China, which a few years ago was uninhabited,
" is now filling up with Chinese. The number of sons of
" the flowery kingdom who emigrated to that point and to
" Singapore, amounted to 100,000 in 1882, to 150,000 in
" 1883, and last year an important increase in these
" numbers was expected. The Draconian laws, through
" which efforts have been made in California and Australia
" to get rid of this inconvenient opposition, are well
" known. These laws, that stand in glaring contradiction
" to the philosophic principles of equality and fraternity
" among all races, despite all efforts to maintain their
" efficiency, remain a dead letter. I never met more Chinese
" in San Francisco than I did last summer, and in Australia
" the Chinese demand is ever increasing in importance. To
" a man who will do the same work for half-price all doors
" are open. Even in the South Sea Islands, the influence
" of Chinese labour is already felt. The important trade of
" the Gilbert Islands is in the hands of a Chinese firm. On
" the Sandwich Islands, the sons of the middle kingdom are

" spreading every year. The North Americans, until now
" the rulers of that island under the native kings of Hawaii,
" are already feeling the earth shaking beneath their feet as
" in vain they resist their inroads. All these things I have
" seen with my own eyes, excepting in Chili and Peru,
" countries that I did not visit. From official documents,
" however, I extract the fact that since 1860 200,000
" Chinese have landed there, an enormous number con-
" sidering the small European population in these countries.
" Europe with her 300,000,000, China with her 400,000,000,
" represent, with the exception of India, the two most over-
" populated parts of the world. Both send their sons to
" foreign climes. They consist of two mighty streams, of
" which one is white and the other yellow. In the annals
" of history, there is no mention of such immense masses of
" people. A series of questions now arises. How will the
" states of the old continent be affected by the emigration
" of so many of its sons ? Now suffering from a plethora
" after such a severe fleecing, will Europe remain in a full
" healthy condition, or similar to Spain, will she lapse into
" a state of anemia ? Who can tell ? What fate is in store
" for the young, rising, aspiring powers of Central Asia,
" that are neither kingdoms nor republics, and what will be
" the reactionary effect on the mother country and on
" Europe ? We do not know. What will be the result of
" the meeting of these white and yellow streams ? Will
" they flow peacefully in parallel lines in their respective
" channels, or will their commingling lead to chaotic events ?
" We cannot tell. Will Christian society and Christian

"civilization in their present form disappear, or will they emerge victorious from the conflict, carrying their living, fruitful, everlasting principles to all the corners of the earth ? We cannot know. These are the unsolved problems, the secrets of the future hidden within the womb of time. What we now distinguish is only the first overture of the great drama of the coming times. The curtain is not yet rung up, and the plot is only to be worked out in the twentieth century."

Mr. Hayter, the Government Statist of Victoria, and the highest authority on such matters in Australasia, has just issued his computation, from which it appears there are but 31,000 Chinese in all Australia, while the Europeans number nearly 3,000,000. Far from the Chinese pouring into that continent in ever-increasing swarms, they have steadily decreased in number ever since the yield of gold began to fall off.

Australia is half as large again as the Chinese Empire proper, nearly as large as the continent of Europe; in spite of all the foregoing reassuring statistics, there is an absolute panic in America and Australia at this moment on the subject of Chinese immigration; both countries have now refused to receive Chinamen as immigrants or otherwise, on any terms whatever.

An American, whose opinion was of some value, said to me, " The real difficulty is that the Chinese do not make citizens; America wants citizens." A Chinaman's only thought is to collect money in order to return with it to China. Even his body, if he dies, must go back there.

CHAPTER X.

SAN FRANCISCO—MONTEREY—JOURNEY TO VANCOUVER.

"Looking seaward o'er the sand-hills, stands the fortress, old and quaint,
By the San Francisco friars lifted to their patron saint."
Bret Harte.

San Francisco, July 31st.—Algernon went to the Presidio, the military station, which is at Fort Point, and from there had a fine view of the harbour.

We visited the mint, and saw $10 pieces being made, also saw some bars of gold worth £2000 each which had just come out of the moulds. While waiting to be taken round we were amusing ourselves looking at the cases of old coins, when I heard an authoritative voice behind me addressing me thus, "What is that coin?" and turning to reply, I saw a tall, powerful-looking woman. I wondered who and what she might be, and was presently told that she was a well-known lawyer in San Francisco. She looked as if she could argue any point to its bitter end.

We also visited the mission church of Dolores, the first church built in California; it was erected in 1776, and is consequently the oldest building here. The little whitewashed chapel did not impress me much, and the altars were gaudy with paper flowers.

Sir Francis Dr..'.e sailed along the Californian coast in 1579, but historians do not agree as to whether he discovered the bay of San Francisco or not. For some unexplained cause, no settlement resulted from this expedition, the first being made by Gaspar de Portales at San Diego in 1769. He, with Father Yunipera Lorra, founded a mission there, erected a cross at Monterey, and continuing their journey northwards, by the merest accident came on the now world-famed bay of San Francisco, so named by them after San Francisco d'Assisi, the founder of the order of Franciscans.

As we were passing quietly along the street we heard the alarm sound at the fire station, it being 12 o'clock, at which hour the engine horses are trained to do as follows :— The moment the alarm sounds, the horses gallop into their places at the engine in readiness to start for a fire. During the night, if warned by the electric bell, in twenty seconds from the time they hear it the engine is off. By cleverly devised mechanism the harness is balanced over the horses in their stalls, the bell communicates with an electric wire, which instantly drops the harness on the horses; they, knowing the sound of the alarm, at once gallop to the engine. The men kindly sounded the gong for us a second time, the horses snorted with excitement and galloped for their places, two for the engine, the others for the salvage carriage, and one of the firemen assured me that on a dark night they looked round for the light of the fire as they galloped along. Charming horses they were, of the Shire breed, and strong, powerful animals.

An old engine-horse who had been so hurt last winter, by falling into a drain on his way to a fire, as to be unfit for engine work, was changed into the salvage carriage, to which he strongly objected, and still always galloped to the engine if he got a chance. The fireman told me it was easy to teach a new horse his place, but always difficult to make an old one change his position.

In the larger stations the men come down a pole from their rooms to their places on the engine, electric wires jerk the blankets off their beds, and this awakes them. One pull draws on their clothes and boots, and two buttons seem to fix all their garments.

Woodward's Gardens, which we visited, used to be well kept; but we found them in a miserable state. The gardens were pretty, but to see the poor animals, dirty, neglected, and half-starved, made me quite unhappy; so much so that I wrote a protest in the form of a letter to the editor of the leading newspaper. We hear the advantages of a free press, but the letter on behalf of the dumb sufferers, whose condition I was anxious to ameliorate, never appeared.

We went to see the Mission Schools for Chinese children at 933, Sacramento Street. I was assured by many people, who seemed to know everything else about San Francisco, that there were no Christian schools for Chinese children in this place. We saw twenty-one girls here, many of them placed in this Mission by the Society for the Prevention of Cruelty to Children. They appeared to be intelligent, and sang several English hymns very nicely, some of them speaking English with a good accent. Several of the older girls seemed stupified by the ill-treatment they had received during a life of shame and ill-usage in the dens of the Chinese quarter. One poor creature, quite blind and deeply scarred with small-pox, sat and wept silently in the corner. I thought—

"He's true to God who's true to man; wherever wrong is done,
To the humblest and the weakest, 'neath the all-beholding sun,
That wrong is also done to us; and they are slaves most base,
Whose love of right is for themselves, and not for all their race."

These children are supported and educated at the expense of different churches in England.

One incident rather amused me in connection with our visit to this mission. A lady, whose name I do not even remember, who sat near us at dinner at the Occidental Hotel, asked if she might come with me to visit the school. She came; and when we were leaving, I thanked the matron, and told her how deeply interested we were with all we had seen. My newly-made acquaintance followed, and I heard her thank the matron for "such an elegant entertainment!" There are several other mission schools for Chinese children, the addresses of which I give below.*

* Methodist Mission, 916, Washington Street; Baptist Mission, Sacramento Street; Miss E. R. Cable's Mission, 810, Central Avenue.

One could spend a long time in San Francisco without seeing everything. Alas! our time is nearly over. We leave to-morrow for Monterey.

August 2nd.—Spent our afternoon at the Cliff House, going there by the new railway, which winds like a snake along the edge of the cliff. As we came near our destination we were far above the sea, and as we peered down into the depths below, and saw the billows rolling in against these great precipices, though the scene was quite beautiful, our sensations were not altogether pleasing. One might have a magnificent view of London if suspended on a scaffolding from the dome of St. Paul's. Our feelings were something similar to what this experience would be.

To-day I wanted nothing better than to sit on the seashore and enjoy myself; and surely there never were more wondrous tints in the breaking waves than there were on this August afternoon; and the corals, the brightly-tinted shells, and the seaweeds each had a little lesson of nature to give me as I sat silently there.

> " Our hearts are one with the sunlit scene,
>   With the sounds that fill the generous air;
> With the seaweeds purple, and brown, and green,
>   With the delicate sandflowers blooming there,
>   With the pink and white shells which lie at our feet."

The docks here are worth a visit, and from them you can see steamers starting for every part of the world.

We were much pleased with the Occidental Hotel; it was both comfortable and quiet. We had good rooms, the table was excellent, the charges moderate, and the manager, Major Hooper, most civil. Fruit and flowers were sent daily to our rooms, and when we left, a beautiful bouquet of pink roses was given to me.

One night, for dinner, Major Hooper ordered for us a dish of "Pamelos," excellent fish which are only found in the bay of San Francisco, and are considered a great delicacy. These fish were about the size of a whiting, and their flavour reminded me of whitebait.

Hotel Del Monti, Monterey, August 4th.—A four hours' journey from San Francisco brought us to this place. The train passed through pretty country; for on this white-looking sandy soil anything will grow if it is irrigated.

The evergreen oaks here take the place of olive-trees; the latter are only beginning to be cultivated here. The oak's foliage, at a little distance, did not look unlike the olive, and the soft grey colouring blended well with the intensely blue sky. The pasture appeared dried up for lack of moisture; still the cattle fed, and seemed to thrive. In the fields of Indian corn, many of which we passed, was the only richly-coloured green we saw during our journey. Horses and cattle gladly eat the leaves of this plant.

Before reaching Monterey, our train plunged into a long cañon, and on emerging from it we found ourselves at the station of Del Monti. The hotel stands in lovely gardens, and is a favourite resort of the people of San Francisco.

We brought with us an introduction to Mr. Charles Crocker, who was most civil to us; but he was in very bad health at the time, and died shortly afterwards.

The bathing here was excellent, only more people bathe in the large baths than in the sea. It was very amusing looking on. Many of the girls were good swimmers and some of the men dived well. The most energetic of the bathers generally swam out to the end of the Pier in the sea after having been in the baths; we saw them capitally from our position above. The bathers have much to learn from Trouville in the way of bathing-dresses, all those worn here being of dark blue with stockinged feet, the only touch of colour were the red caps. The men displayed greater variety in their costumes. When on the pier we saw a somewhat curious sight. The water was very clear, and in it we watched large shoals of sardines pursued by mackerel. The shoals seemed to us about twenty yards in diameter, and circular in shape, and the sardines on the outside were always swimming towards the centre in their endeavours to get into safety, and so constantly pushing those already there to the outside. This gave a curiously regular movement to the whole shoal.

We went for a long drive in the afternoon by the shore, and saw the Cypress Grove (*Cupressus macrocarpa*), the only existing one in the world of this variety. The trees, which stand in a very exposed position, are twisted into

K

all sorts of capricious shapes by the winds of the Pacific Ocean.

Grey, the Botanist, visited this Cypress Grove, and saw also the Monterey Pine (*Pinus insignis*); he said they were both indigenous to this place only. Many are now sent to all parts of the world, and Monterey Pines are being planted extensively on the sandy plains of California, their principal merit being that they grow in almost pure sand.

The Cypress Grove was beautiful, but very difficult to sketch. A sad accident happened while we were there. A good pair of horses had brought us from the hotel, the stupid driver tied them up by the head to one of the cypress-trees, and there left them to their own devices. One of them evidently attempted to roll, and getting the bridle in some way caught up in a branch broke his neck. My attention was attracted in that direction while I was sketching, and seeing the poor horse down, I ran as quickly as I could to his aid; but he was dead. When the driver came he was much annoyed, and would, if he could, have gladly blamed us for his own stupidity. We sent him back to the hotel for another horse, whilst we had lunch in one of the sheltered coves.

The rocks here are covered with masses of bright-coloured seaweeds, and many large sea-birds flew lazily over our heads; as we passed along there were several little Chinese camps at different places near the road; at these, baskets full of polished Ebluna shells were being sold: these shells are of beautiful pink and green shades inside.

They were five cents per shell; and the lady, with whom I was driving bought 200 to decorate the cornice of one of her rooms in New York. The fish that inhabit these shells, after being dried in the sun, are an article of export to China. I was very tired after finishing packing for our departure at 6 A.M. on the morrow.

We spent the next day at San Francisco, and received the greatest attention and civility from the manager of the Occidental Hotel; and when we left that evening he kindly packed three baskets for us, one of wine, one of fruit, and one of luncheon. Nothing was forgotten in our luncheon basket, even table napkins were included; these were Chinese, of curious coloured paper.

The journey was long, hot, and dusty, and we fully appreciated the contents of the baskets before we arrived at Portland, Oregon, which we did the third day after starting.

On leaving Portland we found the cars very much crowded, as there had been a meeting of the Teachers' Association, and many of the women were returning home.

Algernon and I could only secure two upper berths away from each other; and as I had a man sleeping below me, I had to go to bed at 8.30 before he "turned in," and I had to get up at 4 A.M. before he "turned out," at which time I climbed down the ladder with the assistance of the black porter. I doubt if those who boast of the comforts of American travelling have ever tried one hot and dusty night in crowded cars.

We spent a few hours at Tacoma, and were glad to get into a capital cabin on board the Puget Sound steamer for Vancouver, B.C., the door of which opened on to the outer deck, so that we could sit in our cabin and enjoy the view and fresh air, which was delightful after the heated cars.

Puget Sound seemed prettier to-day than when we were going south. Then we had been living in the beautiful woods, now we were returning from Oregon, where all was dried up with the hot sun, and so the fresh pine woods looked green and lovely.

We were amused by a half-grown raccoon which was on the upper deck; he made a curious little cry as he tried to escape from a box to which he was tied by a thong. These creatures are easily tamed, and make rather amusing pets, but this half-wild one seemed very unhappy.

We were much pleased to arrive at Vancouver, where we found thirty-six letters waiting for us at the hotel; in Canada letters follow one from place to place without extra charge for postage.

CHAPTER XI.

VANCOUVER—CANOEING IN HOWE SOUND.

"Made at night a lodge of branches,
And a bed with boughs of hemlock,
And a fire before the doorway,
With the dry cones of the pine-trees."—*Longfellow.*

Canadian Pacific Hotel, Vancouver, British Columbia, August 12*th.*—Very much tired after our long journey. This being Sunday we went to the Scotch Church close to the hotel in the afternoon. Rather a dismal service, and each time I leaned back my cloak adhered firmly to the newly-varnished seat.

In the evening we sat in the wide verandah of the hotel, and had a glorious view of the Sound and the mountains beyond, by pale clear moonlight.

As I recalled the day of the month, it seemed to bring a whiff of the Scotch mountains and heather; we thought of many friends far off in Scotland, not shooting grouse, however, until to-morrow, as it is Sunday.

How one dreams in the moonlight, and through the

mists of time, thoughts of childhood, recollections, impressions, how they crowd into one's mind, and things long forgotten are recalled as if they had happened but yesterday!

August 13*th*.—We drove round the park at Vancouver, the roads of which are being made, and visited the big trees, which are certainly magnificent, one cedar being 50 feet in circumference, a Douglas pine 44 feet, and the largest existing spruce 38 feet, all measured 6 feet from the ground.* These trees are extraordinary, not only from their great girth, but from their enormous height. The Sequoiæ of California are of course much larger, but are a perfectly different variety of tree. I doubt if there exist anywhere larger specimens of the three previously named.

We saw during our drive no less than six eagles' nests.

All along the Puget Sound and round this place sawmills are busy at work. Already the merchants of Australia, Chili, Peru, China, the United States, and Great Britain have discovered that in British Columbia they can obtain a class of timber no other country can supply: red, yellow, and white pine, cedar, hemlock, spruce, larch, and fir, and all of a size that is unrivalled elsewhere.

No one can estimate the enormous amount of timber in this province; it covers the whole of the country one may say up to the snow-line, an area larger than France and the British Isles combined.

* These large trees generally grow in groups of three.

Where was formerly primeval forest, the town of Vancouver now stands, with carpenters, stonemasons, and bricklayers all hard at work increasing its size every day.

The hotel is the principal building in the town, whilst scattered round are some nice houses, a few streets, many building-lots, and much waste land for sale.

Without having seen the forest in its wild state, one cannot understand the amount of labour necessary to bring a "building lot" into condition. Each of the large stumps left in the ground when a tree is felled costs $30 to remove. They have partly to be burnt, partly blown out with giant powder and the rest dug out with picks. To clear one small building lot costs $300. Speculators in such lots, are asking very large prices, which we are told are still going up. We saw a lot which had just been sold for $5000, with only room for one small house between two already built on adjacent ground, and called Mr. Van Horne's and Lord Durham's lots after their respective owners. Vancouver will some day hold an important position, being the railway terminus, and a starting-point to all parts of the world.

We went across the inlet in a row-boat to visit the Indian village which we had only seen before in the distance, when, as we looked across the inlet from the hotel, its little white houses and church glistened in the morning sun. We had considerable trouble in crossing, owing to the tide, which runs in and out very quickly, and on reaching the other side we fastened the boat, and walked through the village, which seemed clean and quiet.

Most of the men were away, but we found two busily engaged making a dug-out canoe, which they were scooping out. One of the Indians looked old and wrinkled, but the other seemed young and active. With the assistance of an Indian boy who understood a little English, Algernon inquired if there was a hunter there who could go after sheep and goat with him. They only shook their heads and said they knew of no one. Many children were playing about, and six squaws were sitting together, making rather a nice screen with tabs of woollen cloth. They all appeared to be amused by our visit; they seemed happy and contented and looked up lazily as we passed. The Mission is Roman Catholic and the church also. On Sundays a priest comes to take the services; on week days, we were told, they were conducted by the schoolmaster. The inside of the church was clean and tidy; these people look after it themselves. Poor simple souls! they seem to have grasped the truth, that there is One who came to save all who believe in Him.

The Indians in this village earn a good living by lumbering, nearly all the men working in saw-mills not far from here.

The evening was beautiful, not a ripple stirred the water, and the mountains were glorious. Our pleasure was rather marred by four stupid men in a boat, who fired in the direction we were going, and several bullets fell close to us; they were too far off to hear our remonstrances, but as every one possesses firearms here, naturally they fall into the hands of many who do not understand how to use them with safety to others.

Blasting goes on daily at Vancouver, and few precautions are taken to warn passers-by. A man was killed last week in this way. The workmen get so accustomed to the use of these dangerous explosives that they leave them lying about. Two days ago enough giant powder was found close to the hotel to have blown up the whole town, but it did not excite much attention; we were told it belonged to the men making roads.

Vancouver is full of the most eminent lawyers in Canada; an important case is proceeding: "The Government of Canada v. The Canadian Pacific Railway." The part of the line made by the Government was to be given over to the Canadian Pacific Railway Company at a certain date, and was to be built up to the standard of the Union Pacific line. The Canadian Pacific Railway Company now maintain that the line is not up to the promised standard. This case will involve an expense of $6,000,000 to the losing side, so all the best legal advice has been procured by both parties. I was told by several of the leading men engaged, that it had entailed tremendous labour for them to learn all the railway terms and slang, which it was absolutely necessary for them to do, in order to examine and understand witnesses.*

We looked into the Court and heard some cross-

* I understand this case is still proceeding.

examination going on, and were also shown photographs of portions of the line said to be unsafe. However, the President of the Canadian Pacific Railway is reported to have come through the mountains, the whole way, going at the rate of fifty miles an hour; this does not look as if he were afraid about the state of the line.

Bears are frequently met with in the forest between Vancouver and New Westminster; we drove that way, and Algernon took his rifle, but we saw no wild animals of any kind. The forest is so dense in some parts it looked as if a way could hardly be forced through it. Everywhere a profusion of wild berries of all kinds is found: raspberries, their canes 18 feet high, salmonberries, blueberries, and cranberries, and these are what attract the bears. During our drive we saw trees said to be 280 feet high; most of the road was an old corduroy one, and we bumped along all the time, taking much interest in what we saw.

August 14*th*.—We were invited to join a party going up the inlet called the "North Arm."

At the entrance of the harbour on the rocks, lay the wreck of the old Hudson's Bay steamer *Beaver*, the first steamboat that rounded Cape Horn, and this she did in 1837. A queer-looking craft she was, and hardly the size of a small steam-tug. The quick running tide had put her on the rocks, and there she will lie until she falls to pieces.

A CANOE EXPEDITION.

We crossed to Moodyville, and saw the large saw-mills at work, and then steamed for twelve miles up the inlet, until we were in impressive solitudes and amidst grand wooded mountains, the distance fading into intense depths of blue. On our way back we saw a glorious sunset, lighting up all the mountains.

August 15*th*.—We prepared for our canoe expedition to Howe Sound.

August 17*th*.—We were to start from False Creek, half a mile from the hotel. On reaching the shore at 7 A.M. yesterday, we saw the Indian's canoe anchored on the other side of the creek; after much calling and whistling, our Indian (William by name) came out of his house, and through Algernon's stalking-glass we saw him packing in all haste, with the assistance of his "*clootchman*" (Chinook for woman); at last he came, and we started. Fine weather smiled on us, and in the distance Vancouver Island was visible; thus we crossed to the lighthouse, which is on the other side of the entrance to Buzzards Inlet.

We had received an invitation to breakfast at the lighthouse, near which Mr. O'Brian (an artist) and his sister were living. We found their tent very comfortable, and our morning's sail had given us the best of appetites. They spoke well of the reliability of our Indian, who had once been for six weeks with them. Upon starting again the sea was too rough for me; and I suffered from the effects of the swell. We sailed the whole way, and it was exciting to see our Indian seated in the stern of the canoe, with the sheet in his hand, driving us, as it were, in the direction he wished, and our little narrow canoe, with its big square sail, speeding us through the water so quickly that at times I felt nervous. Algernon and the Indian, however, reassured me. These coast Indians are all good seamen, accustomed to sail their canoes in all sorts of weather, and these dug-outs really float like corks on the water.

The mountains seemed wooded to the very summit on either side, and in the distance we saw some fine snow-peaks.

At 7 o'clock, after twelve hours' sailing, the canoe was drawn up on the banks, and we camped for the night, which would have passed more pleasantly had the mosquitoes left us in peace. It was almost dark by the time supper was ready. Our "menu" for the evening was as follows: hot bread, tea, bacon, cold chicken, salt beef, and baked potatoes; so we did not starve. Our camp was beside a small stream, and facing us was one of the great islands in the sound.

Our Indian is a good specimen of what an Indian can be when compelled to work for himself. He is bright, intelligent, with good manners, and his camping-kit was so complete as to be far better than our own, for he had a pillow, and white sheets to sleep in, under the sky of heaven. Also he possessed a leather bag, a looking-glass, a brush and comb, and occasionally he put on a pair of new boots. We had brush and comb, but no sheets, pillows, or looking-glass! Whenever he did put on his new boots, then occasion or fancy led him into the water, and so the boots got soaked!

Over the camp-fire, William told us a bear story, and this is word for word as I heard it from him:—

"Indian go after wild sheep, see bear. Him shoot "bear with shot-gun, once, twice; still bear come on. "Indian get out knife, still bear come. Bear catch him, "go, bite, bite, bite! Indian up arms, scratch him, bite, "bite, bite! Indian get knife into bear. Bear thinks "man dead, goes and sits not far off. Indian very sick, "watch bear. Bear watch man too much. Man load gun "again. Bear looks, man shoot again, kill bear. Man "very sick, get back camp all blood!"

Algernon fished with small success, only getting one trout for supper. We saw another. Our Indian ran down to a shallow place, and with a long pole with gaff attached, secured him; but alas! the new boots were in the water several times.

We spent Sunday in camp, and I read the Psalms for the day to Algernon and the Indian, and the latter drew nearer to listen.

"The high hills are a refuge for the wild goats, and the rocks for the conies."

"He appointed the moon for seasons, the sun knoweth his going down."

"Thou makest darkness, and it is night, wherein all the beasts of the forest do creep forth."

"The young lions roar after their prey, and seek their meat from God."

William tells us he is a Roman Catholic, but in his simplicity thinks all belong to that Church. He says, "Me no able to read, but my boy he learn; he be able to do all that."

Our supper of mutton broth, fried onions, tongue, trout, hot bread and biscuits, was much enjoyed. We were obliged to sleep with a smudge in our tent, as the mosquitoes were so bad. It was made with a few hot cinders covered with green leaves and cedar bark. This soon emitted a smoke, and we slept in peace.

We started on Monday for Squawmish Place, at the head of Howe Sound; it is an Indian reserve. We had no wind, so Algernon and the Indian had to paddle the whole way. The sun was hot, and we were glad to get out of the current (which was strong enough to make the work hard), and into the shadow of the great grey rocks, that were covered with masses of seaweed and mussels which lent them every shade of grey and yellow.

We saw an eagle perched on the top of a Douglas pine; it seemed a long way off, and when Algernon got out his rifle, I did not expect he would hit him, but the royal bird fell, a large one too when extended, and of the white-headed variety. We placed him in the stern of the canoe, intending to bring him back, but alas! the heat of that one day defeated our intentions.

The words of Longfellow came to my mind—

> "And the evening sun descending,
> Set the clouds on fire with redness,
> Burned the broad sky like a prairie,
> Left upon the level water
> One long track and trail of splendour."

On, on they paddled for many a long mile before a suitable resting-place was found, and the canoe was hauled up for the night. Our camp was perched high up on some rocks among trees, and below us flowed quite a large river. After the tent was pitched, we went off fishing for a couple of hours. No success. The Indian said, "Salmon not come yet," and it did not seem that they had. We then amused ourselves trying to shoot seals. They were wary and would not allow the canoe within 200 yards of them, but when far enough away to feel secure, they kept bobbing their heads up and down in a very aggravating manner; but happily it is not always necessary to one's enjoyment that one should kill. Men who are excellent sportsmen have told me that some of their pleasantest days after game have been those when success has not crowned their efforts, though they have been enabled to learn something new about the habits of the animals they have been in pursuit of.

After an excellent supper "turned in," but not to sleep, as it was now the mosquitoes' turn to have an excellent supper. They were in thousands, and besides these pests we were tormented by sandflies, which got through our blankets and irritated us beyond endurance; so much so that in the middle of the night, we pulled our blankets on to bare rocks, where there was a little wind, and at last slept; but our blankets were quite wet with the heavy dew when we got up at 4 A.M. The high rock that we had chosen overlooked the Sound, and we had a lovely view. Thousands of stars were still twinkling when we started. After paddling and sailing six miles, we camped for breakfast in the most delightful spot; no mosquitoes. Here we remained until next morning, and spent the day exploring the woods, but found no game of any kind. Following the stream about half a mile up the mountain-side, we discovered some natural granite baths filled with icy stream-water. In the springtime doubtless this is a huge mountain torrent.

August 22nd.—A lovely morning. The Indian had breakfast ready at 4.30, when I came out of my tent. We are returning, and this expedition has been somewhat disappointing; firstly, because the salmon had not come into Howe Sound, and secondly, the time is closed for the shooting of mountain sheep and goat till September, and it is somewhat aggravating, for poor Algernon to feel so near and be unable to have a few days after them. Mosquitoes and sandflies have found us out in our retreat here also, and at night we have to cover our faces in silk shirts to defeat them. Oddly enough, we have been travelling about with curious mosquito cages which can be placed round one's head, completely defending it, but having never had any use for them, we left them behind us at Vancouver. Alas! alas!

A LONG PADDLE.

We started with what the Indian called a "*siwash*" wind. Our canoe sailed beautifully. The wind, however, soon dropped, and so Algernon and the Indian had to do a long day's paddling. We stopped for two hours, going ashore at a pretty spot where there was a creek and lots of good water. The Indian and I prepared dinner, while Algernon lay on his blankets and enjoyed a rest. They paddled by turns, and at last reached the lighthouse, where the O'Brians invited us to tea in their tent. This we declined; we wished to reach Vancouver by night, and wind and tide being fairly favourable, we went on. The sun beat down on our tired heads as from a furnace, but still they plied their paddles sturdily, and when we reached False Creek we had been for sixteen hours in the canoe; a hard day's work!

August 23rd.—My face was very much swollen from mosquito bites, but carbonate of soda with a little water, dabbed on gently with the aid of a bit of cotton wool, at once removed all irritation. The comforts of a house are indeed great when one has been a week in the open, and after a good night's rest we were quite ourselves again, although the object of our expedition—sport—had not been attained.

CHAPTER XII.

GLACIER HOUSE—THE COLUMBIA RIVER.

"Worth makes the man, the want of it the fellow,
The rest is all but leather and prunella."—*Pope.*

August 24*th.*—We left Vancouver in the afternoon for Glacier House, and from the platform of the last car on the train, looked at the deep ravines and great chasms over which the trestle bridges carried us along the banks of the Fraser river.

The old Cariboo trail winds along the opposite side of the Cañon, in many places passing over wooden cribwork on the edge of the bare rocks, and over this a stage with six horses formerly ran daily, no parapet of any kind protecting the traveller from a fall over the precipices. In the spring of the year the teams were often almost unbroken, and were only induced to go by starting at full gallop. The road at one point (on what is called Jackass Mountain) goes round a corner with a precipice of 1,500 feet sheer below it. No one seems to have thought it dangerous, though more than one bad accident occurred here, and once the stage waggon went right over into the chasm beneath.

The Bishop of Columbia gives an interesting account in his journal of his journey along the old trail when the Cariboo gold-mines were first discovered, and before the staging days, in which he compares his position to a fly upon the face of a perpendicular rock, in this case between 2,000 and 3,000 feet high.

Many a miner lost his life at Jackass Mountain and Nicaragua Slide.

In 1860 all supplies were transported to the mines on the miners' backs or on those of Indians, who carried as much as 100 or 150 lbs. William's Creek sustained 16,000 people, some of whom left with large fortunes. "Cariboo Cameron," a man who worked in the mines in this neighbourhood, took out $100,000 of gold in three months; with the money he built a house in Montreal, and after spending all that he had, came back an old man, and worked as before until his death.

At that time at Cariboo the gold was taken out in immense quantities. Few of the miners would leave their claims in order to obtain the necessaries of life, and $70 worth of gold dust was given for a sack of flour, and so in proportion for every sort of provision.

Before the rush of thieves and adventurers into Cariboo, the miners were so honest that their bags of gold dust were left on the shelves in their shanties. Any traveller might enter these and help himself from the flour bag, or cut himself a slice of bacon—true hospitality thus obtained in the midst of the roughest country. The rush for gold in a short time so changed all these kindly ways, that men had to carry loaded revolvers day and night to protect themselves from robbery and murder. Fourteen men caught red-handed were sent down to Victoria for trial, sentenced to death by Chief Justice Begbie, and hanged. This swift retribution did much good.

The Indians were now on their fishing-grounds, and we saw long rows of smoked salmon drying under wooden sheds, this being their way of preserving it for the winter. Further up the river, Chinamen were washing for gold.

An excellent dinner at North Bend ended the day; had breakfast on the dining-car, and arrived at Glacier House in time for lunch. Here, travelling along the line in their saloon, we met Mr. and Mrs. Abbot and party, whose acquaintance we had made at Vancouver.

The Rev. W. S. Green and the Rev. — Swansey had been at Glacier House since the middle of June. They were making a survey of the glaciers in the Selkirks for the Geographical Society;[*] had seen much while there, and had made several important ascents and crossed many of the glaciers, discovering also a valley hitherto unknown. They experienced considerable difficulty in finding any one to go with them; but during the latter part of the time they were fortunate in securing the services of a miner known as Mountaineering Ben, a fine bold fellow, ready and willing to do whatever he was told, and though

[*] The Rev. W. S. Green has just published a book, "The Selkirk Glaciers."

THE GREAT GLACIER.

of course with no actual knowledge of Alpine climbing, still reliable in emergencies.

On their last trip they had been absent eleven days, and had crossed and surveyed seven glaciers, and were of course far above the snow-line most of the time.

One morning when at breakfast they received a visit from some mountain goats, who almost walked into their camp; needless to add the rifle was unloaded. The mountain goats are fine animals; their heads when seen alone give little idea of their size.

Glacier House is not a good place to hunt from, owing to the number of glaciers in the surrounding mountains. To get to the game, one must cross one or more of them, which is dangerous without roping, and other precautions.

August 25th.—We went with Mr. Green and his friend to the great glacier, and after a walk of two miles came to where the bridge over the creek formerly stood; it is now washed away. We scrambled over as best we could, through water part of the way, Mr. Green in front of me and Algernon behind, and on reaching the glacier, were amply repaid for our walk by the view we had of the moraine and ice caves.

The glacier at the base is half a mile across, and five to eight miles long, and from this point we could count six others. Mr. Green told us that he had discovered one larger than this, and that it will be called the Marian Glacier.

Mr. Green was marking the stones at the base of the

glacier to see at what pace it was advancing or receding; and for this purpose he and his friend had to cross it several hundred feet above, to fix poles into the ice at different points. They wished us to go with them, and with such efficient guides, armed with ice axes and ropes, I was most anxious to try it. Algernon, however, objected. I had no proper nails in my shoes, and would knock myself up. So we watched them instead, but it was not the same excitement. They returned in about three hours, and on our way down to the hotel, measured a huge boulder of rock which had been carried there by the ice ages ago. It was 50 × 33 × 34 feet. Another boulder we measured was 91 × 44 × 40 feet. This was the largest carried by ice which Mr. Green had seen during his visit to the Selkirks.

Most pleasant companions were these two Irish clergymen, and great travellers. Mr. G. had made many important Alpine ascents, had visited the West Indies and New Zealand on scientific expeditions, and had been one of those selected for the Deep Sea Commission, so he told us many things which interested and amused us, and our time together passed very agreeably. He related to us, that when in the West Indies, where five varieties of oranges grow and quantities of sugar-cane, he was amused to find all marmalade was made either by Crosse and Blackwell or Keiller of Dundee, for which luxury they paid four shillings a pot.

When in the same place, he heard much of a Frenchman who had a sugar plantation near the coast, and was living in the bay where Columbus first landed, and where he was said to have lost the anchor of his ship. This enterprising Frenchman sought long, hoping to discover its whereabouts, and at last found an anchor which he supposed was the one belonging to the explorer.

Mr. G. drove fifteen miles to see it; but, alas, the anchor was that of a 1000-ton ship: nevertheless, a portrait of the Frenchman, with his name, appeared in the papers of the Geographical Society of Paris shortly after, claiming for him the interesting discovery!

The Canadian Pacific Railway Company have built a charming hotel here, small, but comfortable, and the scenery among these glorious snow-clad mountains is of great grandeur and beauty. In the distance on every side there are glaciers; the valleys clad with pine-trees give warmth to the scene, and the exhilarating effect of the mountain air makes one ready to undertake anything.

There was a small bear at the hotel, and he was an exceedingly good-tempered, funny little animal. I brought him some bunches of blueberries, and he picked off the fruit with evident enjoyment.

The tracks of a grizzly were seen the day before on the trail, two miles off; they were about a foot long. Algernon spent two days in trying to get him, but with no success. Two black bear have been shot within three miles of Glacier House this season.

As I was sketching to-day, some navvies passed the place where I was sitting. It was Saturday evening, and the men had just been paid their week's wages.

Two of them had evidently been drinking, so I half closed my portfolio, as I did not wish to run the chance of their stopping to talk to me. They went on, but the next two stayed, and appeared anxious to see what I was doing. They were sober, so I went on painting. They looked with much interest at my sketch; and one of them said: "I wish to buy that picture." I told him that I did not sell my sketches, but painted merely for my own amusement; but that there was an artist staying in the hotel who had some very nice pictures of the places round. "I've seen his," the man replied, "but I like yours best; why won't you sell me this one? Name your own price." The man's evident desire to have the sketch pleased me, and, to make a long story short, I said I would give it to him. To this he said "No; I won't take it for nothing."

He was so anxious to come to some arrangement about it, that at last I said: "If you will send some money to the Hospital (which has been opened for railway employés at Donald) you shall have the picture." He promised he would come next day to settle about it; but we left by the mid-day train, and he had not then arrived.*

The men get excellent wages, working on the railway—some as much as two and even three dollars a day; and as they have no other means of spending their money, those who do not save spend it, alas! at the

* Months afterwards I heard he had come that evening, and was much disappointed; but as I did not know his name, I could then do nothing.

saloons and drinking-bars. Books and newspapers, we always found, were very welcome.

We travelled from Vancouver with the Head Master of the Brighton Grammar School, who told us he had made arrangements to send the men books from home. He and a friend had been out in Canada to visit some of their old school-boys, having been anxious to see for themselves if they had deteriorated among their rough surroundings. Evidently they had found this to be the case in some instances. He lectured much to working-men, and seemed to take great interest in everything he heard about the country and settlers.

We had to leave Glacier House on Sunday evening for Golden City, and passing the Beaver and Kicking-Horse Rivers, which were both in flood from heavy rain, we found our train suddenly brought to a stand-still. A tree had fallen across the line, but it was soon removed with the help of an axe, and on we went.

At Golden City we found Captain Armstrong, of the steamer *Duchess*, waiting for us at the station with a waggon; we were ere long settled on board, with the best cabin placed at our disposal. The *Duchess* was built owing to the enterprise of several Englishmen, and many persons travelling in Canada will doubtless gladly avail themselves of this means of seeing the Rocky Mountains and Selkirks from the Columbia River.

There is also a trail this way by which one can get into the United States territory at a place called Sandy Point

Station on the Northern Pacific Railway. Of course such an expedition requires Indian guides and good ponies, and would take about twelve or fourteen days.

At last we were off. We started early in the morning, and for several hours passengers and freight kept joining the steamer. About twelve persons sat down to dinner. Some of the men looked rough and unkempt, others always seemed to prefer coming when everyone else had gone away. A Chinaman waited, and the cook was also Chinese. The food, which was excellent, was brought up from below on a primitive sort of "lift," or what would be called in this country an "elevator." I was quite anxious about the Chinese boy who waited; he had an awkward way of putting his head instead of the dishes into the lift, and that this portion of his body remained in its proper place was solely by the favour of fortune! It was only a question of time when he should lose his head if he remained possessed of his ill-placed confidence in the lift.

Captain Armstrong told us he had a very fine-looking Indian for a time as servant, but he was photographed frequently without his knowledge, and the last time cleaning boots and knives. A picture of him in this menial capacity was too much for his pride; next day, the first time the steamer stopped, he left never to return.

The principal tribes here are the Kootenays and Shuswhaps; the latter came originally from near Cariboo. There are about 500 Kootenays and 100 Shuswhaps in this district. When the Commissioners came to allot them reservations, for several years they refused them, their

chief saying, "Our land extends from the boundaries of the United States to the Rocky Mountains. Let the white men come if they will; we shall not interfere with them." And they kept their word. But as time passed, and they understood better the chances of being crowded out, they accepted reservations, but they do not receive rations, and do not feel bound to live on their reservations.

Several times have the white settlers been completely in the power of these Indians, who have always behaved well. I will give one example of the way troubles arose.

A miner who thought he was being robbed watched his gold night and day. A Kootenay Indian with his bride were passing; he had not been concerned in the robbery, but lifted a nugget of gold to show his bride. The miner fired, the Kootenay was wounded, drew his knife, and made for the miner, who fired three times before killing his victim. The tribe rose, and, surrounding the miners, could easily have annihilated them. Their chief showed great patience, **demanded the hanging** of the murderer only, and finally consented to let his trial come off at Victoria, B.C. Indians went down as witnesses. The white man got off, and now keeps a bar at Esquimault, but in the Kootenay country his life would not be worth an hour's purchase.

The Kootenays like ranching, and own about 1,000 head of cattle. They take little or no interest in mining, and none of these tribes have any gold ornaments. The name of the last good Kootenay chief was Michael; he died eight years ago. The present chief is inferior to him in every way.

The punishment given to squaws who have given offence to the tribe, is to fell a large pine-tree with nothing but a small tomahawk, and as they do almost all the manual labour this seems to me very hard on them.

The mounted police, commanded by Major Steel, have just been removed from this valley. Seventy-five men were here. These were necessary where many interests had to be considered; but the Government of British Columbia did not care to pay for their support, so they were removed.

Major Steel was liked and respected by the Indians; they always told him the truth, and knew he wished to deal fairly and impartially with them. Alas! that there are not more who command their esteem and respect. They find white men every day trying to get the better of them, and treating them in a way which is a disgrace to civilization.

Mining is the great attraction in the Kootenay district. Mines of inexhaustible wealth are always supposed to be waiting for the mining adventurer, and no doubt some are found; but there is generally the difficulty of want of capital to develop them. During the summer miners take up other work, so as to be able to spend the winter on their claims.

I noticed a fine-looking young fellow on the boat, dressed in the costume of the country, blue overalls, long boots, blue shirt all embroidered and laced up the front, and a cowboy's hat; his nice open and good-tempered-looking face made me wish to speak to him. An opportunity soon occurred. He was going to shoot a duck, but found he had no cartridge in his rifle. I said it was a pity. He seemed pleased when I addressed him, and told me the old story. He had been prospecting, had found a galena-mine, and pointed out a mountain in the distance where his treasure was, but he had no money to work it. He and a friend toiled at it in the winter; in the fall (as the autumn is called here) he made money by carrying freight up and down the river, after the steamer had stopped running.

Four men rowing brought up their boat, with 2,000 lbs. of stuff on board, 100 miles up stream in four days. One load generally paid them from $100 to $115, but often they had to start with only half a load.

He had been out here five years, and liked the life, had just built himself a new boat, and hoped to make his first trip in her shortly.

Later in the day Captain Armstrong said to me, "I will point you out one of the best specimens I know of a 'Western man,'" and directed my attention to the young fellow to whom I had been speaking. He also said, "He is the strongest and one of the most determined men in the valley, and will make his way."

Until lately both passengers' tickets and freight were paid for either in nuggets or gold dust. We saw a 2-oz. nugget, worth £7, which the Captain had just obtained.

A few days before we came up, Captain Armstrong sent a 50-lb. bag of gold dust to be changed at the bank in Victoria. The gold is so pure it is worth $18 an ounce, and loses very little when smelted.

A smelter is being built at Vancouver, and will prove a great advantage and convenience to miners in Canada and British Columbia, for until now all ore has had to be sent to the States to be smelted, and a heavy duty is required at the frontier.

I sketched for some hours from the deck of the steamer, and left my painting materials there when I went to tea. Algernon was standing near, when a bumptious and very loquacious young man who had come from Ontario came up to him and said, "You are an artist; you seem to paint rather nicely." Algernon was much amused, as painting is not one of his accomplishments, and the speaker looked anything but a capable critic. Appearances are sometimes deceptive!

This reminds me of another occasion, when some friends of ours were travelling on the cars in the usual cowboy's "kit." An elderly gentleman, one of their fellow-travellers, who was anxious to hear all he could about ranching, was told by the porter of the train that he might get all the information he wanted from two cowboys in the smoking-room. These were our two friends, who were not cowboys; but this mistake was likely to occur, as nearly every one dresses in this way.

A very strong-minded American lady was in the train from the Glacier House with us, travelling in the interests of some Boston newspaper. Her appearance would have warranted her being able to travel round the world alone. She had on a short serge dress, her hair was cropped, and at the back of her head she wore a grey wideawake, while her sole ornament was a small liqueur bottle suspended by a silver chain. She kept her note-book and pencil in hand the whole time.

I can't help thinking, as I see all these strange people— miners, boatmen, cowboys, toilers of all kinds—how some are born to fortune and some to toil, and that the majority know little but hard work from their cradles to their graves, and that many of these turn out nobler and better than those who lead lives of luxury and pleasure ; and how work has nearly always a good effect on character, while that of luxury and pleasure is just the contrary.

"Out West" we saw no poor, for all could get work, and there were few idlers. The idlers there were had chosen their lot, being addicted to either drinking or gambling, and when idleness and dissipation mastered them, they would blame fate by saying they were "down in their luck."

We had a lovely trip up the Columbia river. Captain Armstrong was so kind and considerate that, though I was the only woman on board, I did not feel it in the least, and the passengers amused me. They were mostly surveyors, prospectors, and miners. Captain Armstrong told me that there were two parties on board, four men belonging to one and three to the other; that they were going to try which should be the first to stake a claim on a rich galena-mine, which one of the four had discovered. The finder was a drunken, good-for-nothing man. With his party was the nice young fellow I had been speaking to the day before, and two others. These men had promised to help the finder of the mine to establish his claim and their own.

On the opposite side were a mining engineer, a fine-looking big man, who was a miner, and a hanger-on, who had promised to take them to the mine. The latter, having failed to get the drunken discoverer of the mine to tell him where it was, was rather in disgrace with the men with whom he was travelling.

Our steamer stopped for the night, making fast to the bank. The three had horses waiting at this point, and hoped to start at dawn, and so get ahead of the other party. However, when morning came their horses had disappeared, having been let loose by some of the others; so they had to come on board again as far as the next stopping-place, which was ten miles from the coveted mine, over the most unpromising-looking country for a hurried march. Here both parties went ashore, scowling at each other. The four men took a pony and a row-boat off the steamer; we left them all on the bank. I asked Captain Armstrong who would win. He answered, "The young fellow will get there first. Last winter he walked to Golden over a bad trail a distance of thirty miles, stayed there for one hour, and then returned, walking fifty more."

What would not some give to have this splendid

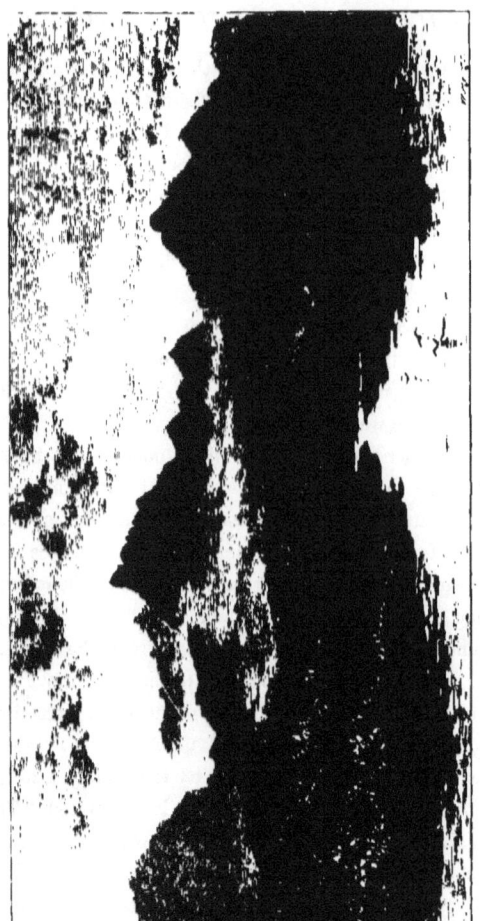

WINDERMERE, BRITISH COLUMBIA.

To face p. 100.

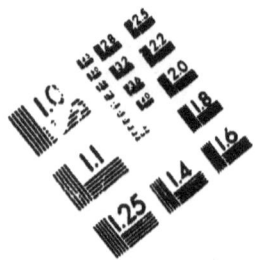 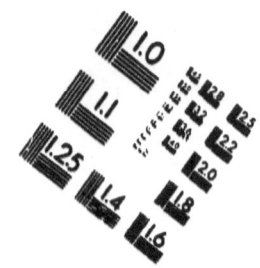

**IMAGE EVALUATION
TEST TARGET (MT-3)**

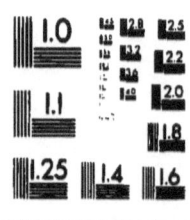

← 6" →

Photographic
Sciences
Corporation

23 WEST MAIN STREET
WEBSTER, N.Y. 14580
(716) 872-4503

strength and energy? I may add that this young fellow did get to the mine first, running on and firing the trail behind him, to delay the opposition party.

After entering the Columbia lake we came to undulating country—excellent grazing-land. We stopped at a landing called Windermere, where a small hotel has lately been built. Two Kootenay Indians were standing by their ponies at the landing, and looked most picturesque; they were the first we had seen.

Before the Canadian Pacific was built, it took eight days with pack-horses to reach this place from Sandpoint, on the Northern Pacific Railway.

It being too late to start for Findlay Creek, we arranged to stay on board for the night, and spent the evening paddling about in a canoe, and shooting a few ducks.

After our return a drunken miner, armed with a Winchester rifle, came on board, and asked first for whisky, and then to stay. Neither of these things would Captain Armstrong allow, so he had to spend the night in the willow-bushes on the bank.

CHAPTER XIII.

Sam's Landing—The Trail to Findlay Creek—The Ponies.

"The hills were brown, the heavens were blue,
A woodpecker pounded a pine-top shell;
While a partridge whistled the whole day through,
For a rabbit to dance in the chapparel,
And a grey grouse drummed 'All's well, All's well.'"
Joaquin Miller.

August 19th, Findlay Creek.—Two miserable-looking Indian ponies were all we could hire. Algernon's was so small it did not look as if it could carry him, but as no others were available we were obliged to make the best of them, and started. The C——s kindly sent a buckboard for our luggage; we took with us only what was absolutely necessary.

The youth from Ontario before mentioned succeeded in obtaining a better pony. He was on his way to a place called Canal Flat, and notwithstanding the advice of more experienced people, fastened his valise behind his saddle, and started at a gallop! We jogged along slowly, and after half-a-mile met him again, this time looking a helpless object. He had had a bad fall. The pony, naturally frightened by the jerking of the valise, had begun bucking, and very soon got rid of his rider. The contents of the valise were strewed over the ground, and a good-natured squaw had caught the pony. There we left him.

Our ponies required a good deal of spur; the Indian to whom they belonged owned 100, but he only caught up a few at a time, and worked them until they were tired out and poor, and then fresh ones took their place; a bad system, and very hard on the ponies.

The country over which we rode was terraced, undulating ground. All through British Columbia these terraces abound, the three successive tiers marking three successive epochs when geological disturbances took place; they are quite uniform, of even surface, and covered with bunch grass and sage brush, being quite free from boulders, while here and there a few scattered pines relieve the yellow bareness so characteristic of this district.

These terraces, Dr. Hector says, are noticeable also on the Athabasca, in California, and in Mexico. Bunch grass only is found growing on them, the peculiar soil formed by the disintegration of limestone or soft volcanic rocks seeming to suit its requirements. One great disadvantage of the bunch grass as food for cattle is that it takes three years to recover after being closely eaten down, and from its mode of growth in distinct tufts, the ground is but scantily covered with herbage; therefore a cattle range must be very extensive, thirty acres not being too much to allow for each beast.

It was refreshing sometimes after riding down-hill to come to a creek with a running stream, and bright-coloured grass; but we quickly left these places behind, and most of our ride lay over dusty plains, with a few pine-trees scattered about, where everything looked dried-up, there not having been rain for two months.

The chirrup of grasshoppers made a cheerful sound, and occasionally from behind a pine-tree, we saw a little chipmunk hurrying off chattering after having a look at us. Pretty little fellows they are, about half the size of a squirrel, with two little stripes down the back.

Our Indian followed us in order to receive payment for the hire of his ponies, and having caught us up gave Algernon his pony, the other being tired out; and continuing our journey until the shadows of evening fell, we at last drew near Findlay Creek. Three or four times during the day we had taken off the saddles and given the ponies a good rest and feed, but as neither of us had tasted food for over twelve hours, we were glad at last to see this wooden house of Findlay Creek, to have a kindly welcome from our friends, and a good tea. Poor Indians! it is shameful to think there are white men who hire their ponies, and then don't pay for them. We heard later that the lad who was bucked off had acted in this way.

This building has been put up since our friends were here last year. It is a board house. Passing into it we found ourselves in the sitting-room, behind which was the kitchen and servant's room; on either side of the sitting-room are two bedrooms, one the C——'s, the other ours. N—— has a tent outside, a short distance from the house. A narrow shelf runs round the sitting-room, three and a half feet from the floor; on it are arranged rows of meat cans, tinned Californian fruits, rifles, cartridges, fishing-rods, and other things, mostly of a sporting character. A stove, a table, some wooden stools, and two hammock chairs, complete the furniture of the room.

The ponies feed around the house, and a cow which has been lent to Adela does likewise; the calf is tethered, but gives us some trouble by constantly getting loose. The fresh milk is a welcome addition to tea, and a daily rice pudding is much appreciated, as milk in these out-of-the-way places is the greatest luxury.

August 20th.—Algernon and N—— went off for a hunt to-day, and expect to get back to-morrow. They packed their blankets, a frying-pan, teapot, and a few other things which they took with them.

August 21st.—Tom C—— left for Calgary this morning, driving on the buckboard, as he had sprained his ankle; the trail is exceedingly rough, so this kind of locomotion is not very comfortable!

Adela and I spent our morning in making pine pillows. First we had to find some stuff to make into cases; a piece of striped window-blind did this. Then we had to fell our pine-trees; it took the needles of three small trees to fill one pillow, but they were most successful when done. The scent of the pine needles has a most soothing effect on the nerves; the only objection to our pillows is their weight.

The hunters have come back tired and hungry. They had seen nothing, not even the track of a deer.

The C——s' ponies escaped to-day; they were loose, to enable them to pick up more food, but two had their lariats trailing. Algernon went off to look for them; he returned in the evening, having been twenty miles in search of them, but finding himself at the Canal Flat, where Baillie Grohman has a store, he purchased two pairs of moccasins, of which he is very proud.

The ponies were caught and brought back, the first one from the upper camp by the Chinese cook; then N—— on this truant (Whitebait by name) found Adela's; and towards evening Pongo, N——'s pony, came to feed, and was speedily captured and picketed.

On the steamer coming up the Columbia, Algernon met a hunter, named Moulson. He knows all this country well, and Algernon would fain have gone hunting with him, but Moulson had unfortunately made his plans for the autumn, so it was impossible. He, however, gave us much information. The distances to get to game seem to me very great; he seemed to think nothing of them, and spoke of carrying his pack of 60 lbs. weight on his back for days together as nothing uncommon.

In the upper Kootenay Lake, which it takes eight days to reach from here with pack-ponies, there is excellent spring fishing. The land-locked salmon is found in these waters, also the red and white charr. The red charr is excellent eating, and is caught up to 20 lbs. weight. In some of the small streams which flow into the Kootenay Lake, is found what the miners call red fish; they are from 3 to 6 inches long, rather flat and very good food. They are spawned one year, and return the following to the same place, spawn, and remain working their way up-stream until they die, the mouth and fins decaying; when washed ashore they are a favourite food for the bears, a number of which frequent these creeks.

Moulson told us the following bear story : In the summer of 1875, on the shores of Ochre Lake, he and a party of miners saw a large grizzly bear. Moulson fired at a distance of 75 yards: the grizzly made for the river, and many shots were fired at him. After swimming the river he was found 500 yards away from the bank, with eighteen shots in him. two of the bullets having gone through his heart; this shows the wonderful vitality of the animal, and the consequent danger of following him when wounded.

The Kettle river, at the foot of the gold range, is also a good place for sport; this same hunter told us he had shot forty-seven deer there one fall.

The upper camp. is about a mile and a half from us, and there the manager and many of the men who are gold-mining live. Adela and I went to see the men working the hydraulic on the river bank; the force of the water is so great that one saw the whole bank crumbling away under its power. They were working to get down to the old bed of the creek, where they expect to find gold in considerable quantities. One of the miners gave us each a large pan of gravel and sand to "pan out," as they call it; we sat down beside a small stream, and proceeded to wash it. This was slow work, as we did not understand how to do it. One has to keep one's pan under the water, and by constantly shaking it, the big stones and gravel come to the top; these must be removed until nothing is left but the black sand; if there be any gold it is found in this deposit. We each spent about an hour and a half over our respective pans, and were rather wet before they were done. I had three colours in mine, Adela two. Colours are small atoms of gold, about the size of a pin's head; three colours in a pan pay for working.

People who ought to know, said there was certainly much gold to be found at Findlay Creek, which extends for eight miles.

Frank, an old French Canadian miner, who helped us with one of the pans, told us a good miner could wash out 125 pans a day, and that they have been paid as much as $6 for each pan. He told us also that he and three other men made $14,000 each in three months. He spent the whole of it in prospecting. Another miner, a friend of his in the States, made $250,000 in seven weeks, went to San Francisco, and spent it all!! Miners seldom save or lay by money to start in other modes of life; easy come, easy go, either in having what they call a good time, or in prospecting for another mine. Cases are too common of miners going into big cities, and in an astonishingly short time, running through incredibly large sums of money.

For three days previous to the 3rd September, I had been feeling very feverish, and rather feared an attack of mountain fever, but quinine averted it.

Algernon and N—— went off that afternoon for some days; they wished to try and find an Indian to hunt with them, and also to buy some ponies for us, and to fetch some provisions.

September 4th.—Adela and I started after lunch to go and fish; only one pony was available, which goes by the name of Whitebait, and if any pony can be like a fish, it is this one, both as regards colour, and a fishy eye of which he is the possessor.

She rode; the trail was very dusty, and after a mile and a half we picketed the pony, and began to fish. They had been working the hydraulic above this place, so we did not get a single rise, and eventually took to sketching. After this we wandered about, finding the single chrysanthemum growing in great abundance, and other flowers also, but heavy drops of rain began to fall, so we started for camp. I rode; we had a very steep ascent to make from the creek, and when we got to the top Adela looked tired. Happy thought! the pony might carry two: I got behind the saddle, the long-suffering Whitebait did not seem to mind; Adela scrambled up in front, and so we rode back to the wooden house. It was rather difficult to keep one's balance without a saddle on the hills and steep banks. Adela suggested, "What if we meet a grizzly!" however, this did not happen, and we got home all right.

Three people arrived to tea from Canal Flat, friends of the B. Grohman's; they were drenched with rain, the two girls having on only their cotton bodices and riding-skirts. It is advisable always to wear flannel shirts and to have warm clothes in this country, as the mornings and evenings are always cold, and chills are apt to bring on mountain fever.

A red lily grows here which is very pretty; we dug up some roots to send home.

September 5th.—Spent the morning at the hydraulic. An Indian arrived with three ponies, two for us, the other for one of the men at the upper camp. Their price was $50 each.

September 6th.—Algernon and N—— returned, both looking rather tired, they had been over eighty miles looking for a half-breed hunter; he has promised to go out with them in three weeks, so in the meantime they have made up their minds to hunt by themselves.

September 7th.—Saddled our ponies and started for Canal Flat; we rode down the trail alongside the creek, which was wild looking with its huge boulders of rock, the trail sometimes being cut out of the face of the cliff high above the stream, whilst the rush of water could be heard in the cañon far below.

We crossed a small flat on which were many deserted log-houses, some with their doors still locked, though their owners would probably never return. One pretty little log-house with a verandah (very likely built years ago by some man who had brought the girl he loved with him, and wished her home to be prettier than the others) stands by itself deserted like the rest; a fine view of the mountains and creek stretching away in the distance before it. They are all gone, the people who built them—and where? only the log-houses remain, dreary and desolate, since the gold rush of 1863, when a quarter of a million of dollars was taken out of the creek.

The ponies stepped carefully over the fallen timber, and we jogged along through pretty woods, passing on our way one or two small lakes, the banks of which were white with alkali. We descended at last by a steep pack-trail to the flat. Gangs of men were working there at the Kootenay Canal, both Chinese and white labourers. This canal was being made to connect the upper Columbia lake and the Kootenay river, and is a work of great enterprise; the only thing that makes one doubtful of its success as a financial speculation is that many men who know every inch of the Kootenay river, say that there are falls lower down, which render it utterly unnavigable. One can hardly believe that men would undertake such an enormous expenditure of money, without first ascertaining this fact, which, if true, would render the canal practically useless.

The Indians seemed much amused with our appearance, and came to the store where we went to buy some things in order to observe us more closely.

We were not much to look at, as Adela and I dressed with regard only to perfect comfort: woollen petticoats and tweed jackets, cowboy hats and long thick boots, the only suitable dress for roughing it out here.

One pretty-looking squaw was what they would call "*heap smart.*" Her bright-coloured blanket thrown gracefully round her active figure, and her embroidered leggings, her moccasins, blue bead necklace, and the gay silk handkerchief which she wore, all formed masses of rich colouring; she, like all Kootenay women, carried her "*quirt*," or riding-whip, for they are horse Indians and rarely walk. All the others sat in groups and chatted in their own tongue.

After a pleasant tea at the Grohmans', the ponies were saddled up, and off we rode again, reaching the wooden house about 8 P.M.

The bunch grass looks dried up and withered, for there is frost at night; still the ponies live on it and flourish, and how patient they are with those terrible black flies, which choose a place on their necks where ponies cannot dislodge them! We find rows of them with their heads buried until the places are raw and bleeding; perhaps this is partly the reason why the poor creatures so love a dust-bath. After they return from a long day's journey they paw up the ground, and then roll where it is soft, and get up a mass of mud and dust; but a few shakes, and they are clean again, as clean as one wants an Indian pony to be.

Adela and I spend a quarter of an hour daily in giving our special favourites a brush-up, and certainly, since they have got over the alarm of seeing women in petticoats attending to them, they are most tractable and quiet, and seem pleased to stand patiently as long as we wish.

All ponies and dogs "out West" seem shy of women. When riding up the trail from Windermere, I caused two mule teams so much alarm by my unusual appearance on a side-saddle, that in order to pacify them, and prevent the waggons from leaving the trail, I had to conceal my objectionable self behind some bushes until they had passed.

September 8th.—Up at 7 A.M. Watered all the ponies with Algernon at the creek close by. I cleaned my boots and mended Algernon's moccasins. My pony went as pack-horse, as we were still short of one, and by 12 o'clock five ponies were saddled and packed and off; they went to bring back provisions for a hunt.

Here most men ride in Californian saddles, for on them a certain amount of "kit" can be packed; they are, however, exceedingly heavy, some of them weighing 38 lbs. When a long journey has to be done, this must be an objection, but they are the only saddles which will stand the rough work of these parts.

Adela and I were only to go half-way down the trail to get letters out of a box which was nailed to a pine-tree there, and was our post-office, and we also hoped to meet Tom C—— on his way back.

The want of books and music we feel much. We have read all the books we have, and a banjo is the only musical instrument that can be carried in the mountains.

The miners have no amusement of any kind. They work hard all the seven days, and seem contented and happy, and one only regrets that so many squander their savings at the first big town they go to after their summer's work is over.

I gave $50 for the white pony at the upper camp to-day, as I did not like the one purchased for Algernon. (And he turned out a really good one, carrying Algernon over the roughest ground and the worst "windfalls" during the time we were in the mountains, without giving him a fall, and on one occasion he took me down the side of a ravine over ground where it looked as if only a goat could have travelled.)

We had the offer of another horse, but did not much fancy him or his owner, the latter being a very rough-looking fellow, who was armed with a revolver and belt full of cartridges. We heard just after that the police were searching for a horse-thief, who had stolen a band of forty horses and brought them into British Columbia from the North-West Territory. We thought most likely this was the man that was wanted; but all the police had left the country, and as Findlay Creek is between the Selkirks and Rockies, the thief was fairly safe, and could easily get off into the States.

All the Government horses are branded on the hoof, and any one found in possession of them, whether thief or not, is fined $50. In many places a horse-thief would be lynched without a trial.

CHAPTER XIV.

FISHING—MINERS—ALGERNON'S DIARY.

"Above the pines the moon was slowly drifting,
 The river sang below;
The dim sierras, far beyond, uplifting
 Their minarets of snow."—*Bret Harte.*

September.—The weather was glorious, and we lived out of doors all the time; some days for hours together I sat on a log, overlooking the valley, and watched the ponies feeding. We were obliged to keep some of them on lariats, because they strayed so much to dig for the roots of the pea-vine, which has a carroty-looking root, that seems to be very nourishing. It smells rather like a bean, and horses are extremely fond of it.

A few days ago our hunters started again at dawn. The animals were brought in, the new purchase—the white pony—mounted and saddled, much to the satisfaction of the owner. Blankets, tent, pots, pans, tin mugs, &c., were all collected, as well as provisions, and one of the miners who helped to pack, showed them how to make " the diamond hitch," a knot specially used for fastening loads on to pack-saddles.

Breakfast bacon had been sent for all the way to Golden City; but one does not always get what one sends for. Bacon was very scarce; a side of horrid-looking, very fat salt pork came instead. N—— sat and looked at it sadly, saying, "How can one eat such stuff;" however, there was nothing to take its place, so it went on the expedition; and, I may add, was thankfully eaten.

All was finally settled, and the hunters said good-bye. N—— and Algernon waved their hands, the kettles rattled, the black horse bucked two or three times, rushed madly forwards, and in a few minutes disappeared into the woods, leaving behind him provisions of all kinds scattered in every direction. We all started in pursuit, and after some time found him with the pack-saddle broken and most of the heavy things lying round him or in his tracks. Half the day was lost before the pack-saddle was mended. N—— this time rode away on the refractory horse, "Pongo" following with the pack-saddle.

In the afternoon I galloped my pony to the upper camp, and returned with 20 lbs. of flour.

The mornings are bitterly cold, but after the sun is up the thermometer sometimes stands at 85° or 90° in the shade, and at night 8° or 9° of frost. The changes of about 70° in the twenty-four hours made me again feel ill. I took quinine and aconite to try to keep off fever, for there is no doctor nearer than Golden City, 150 miles off.

Adela and I consulted the Homœopathic book on fevers of all kinds, and finding my ailments suited all the symptoms, finally decided on perseverance with aconite as a remedy; but I was depressed, and feeling very "down on my luck," and went to bed after a very hot bath. Adela too felt ill with swollen face and tooth-ache. No sooner was I in bed than drip, drip, drip, came the rain through the roof. As I knew that both cold and draughts were to be avoided, and as in spite of all our arrangements the wind was blowing in every direction, I got up, covered the bed with a waterproof, hoisted an umbrella over my head, and having arranged a screen with some shawls, went to sleep, and awoke in the morning much better.

Wrote some letters which had to lie peacefully upon the shelf until there was an opportunity of posting them.

The hunters returned from their three days' trip in the mountains, the trail by which they had hoped to go they found impassable—owing to "windfalls"—without a lot of chopping, and they saw no sign of game.

The first clergyman we had seen since our arrival came to-day, Mr. Irving by name, from Donald, where he had a nice little church; he had just completed the annual tour of his district, which covers an area in British Columbia as large as Scotland, having taken the same pony 780 miles in seven weeks, the animal all the time feeding only on the bunch grass. He told me that the railway hands at Donald had assisted during their spare time in carving all the cedar benches in the little church, and that they had sometimes five short services on Sunday. Donald now has a hospital for the railway-men, who

FINDLAY CREEK. [*To face p.* 178.

unfortunately meet with numerous accidents in the mountainous section of the C.P.R. At first it was defective in many respects, but now the men are well cared for, the nurse being a man who came there as a patient and expressed a wish to remain. There have been as many as twenty-one patients at one time in hospital.

Had a long ride up the valley, and enjoyed a gallop. Saw pretty views of the blue mountains on either side of Findlay Creek, which wended its way through its rocky bed far below us, looking like a silver thread in the bright sunshine. The trail became narrow and difficult as we descended, so much so that a false step on the part of the ponies would have plunged us into the creek far below. We picketed the ponies where they could have a good feed, having first taken off their saddles, then we began to fish.

Such a nice-looking pool at the end of a little rapid, the water of the brightest emerald green. From the rock above, from which I was casting, I saw not only my line and minnow, but also the fish inspecting it: alas! they did not seem to think much of him, so after a few casts I removed him and tried one half his size.

It is quite a fallacy to think that British Columbian trout are easily caught. After looking through my flybook, I selected a small-sized fly with bright hackles, and soon we had nine nice trout on the bank. I now tried a grasshopper; he was too big, so I returned to my fly, and two more fish were added to the basket—quite a pleasant little afternoon's sport.

Last night we were all awakened by the barking of one of the dogs, but as he was always giving false alarms, we shouted to him to keep quiet. Soon, however, we heard some one outside saying, "Paper! letter!" Algernon called Tom C——, and they found an Indian who had ridden up thirty-five miles during the night with a letter. After an hour or two he took the answer back, making seventy-five miles in all, in the dark, over a bad trail part of the way—a good night's work!

Algernon and Tom C—— took a pack-pony down to the flat, to get sugar, tea, and bacon. I went with them a couple of miles, then I stopped to make a sketch, and after two hours resaddled, fastened my drawing-block and other things to my saddle by the buckskin thongs, and galloped back to the house.

Two Indians who had brought potatoes seemed delighted to go on a hunt with Algernon and N——, and accordingly they made up their minds to start at dawn the following day. They were rather fine-looking Indians, and wore their hair long, parted in the middle, and plaited down the sides with beads and ribbons. They wore bead necklaces and leather bracelets, studded with brass nails; also woollen shirts, and tight blanket leggings, fringed, and reaching half way up their thighs, and a blanket fastened round their waists by a cartridge-belt, which also held a large hunting-knife, completed their costume.

The Indians mostly carry their rifles in covers, generally made of buckskin, and often prettily worked with beads. On their feet they wear moccasins; at this time they are all wearing old ones, as the hunting season has just begun, but as soon as they have had time to dress some hides, they will all appear in smart new ones.

September 15*th*.—Algernon, N——, and three Indians, with six horses, one of which carried the pack, started on their hunt to-day.

September 16*th*.—Mr. Irving, who was with us two days ago, held a service at Canal Flat. We hoped to have gone, though it was a ride of over twenty miles, but all the ponies had stampeded except Adela's, and as they were nowhere to be found we had to give it up.

The cold nights seemed somewhat to try the horses. Adela's horse was ill to-day with a swelled throat, which we blistered with mustard. We find that one of the "cayeuses" we bought is well known as a beast that always strays and takes others away with him. An unpleasant discovery!

One of the miners came up to see Tom C——, who was away, and we went out to speak to him. He said, "There is one thing that surprises me about you two ladies."

I asked, "What is that?"

"Well," he said, "I've never before seen any real ladies from the old country, and I always understood that they would not speak to a fellow like me, and behaved so haughty like. Now it's quite different to what I expected with you two ladies; and you are not dressed either as I expected, but William" (a man the C——s had brought from England) "tells me if I saw you in England I should hardly know you—that Lady A—— wears a hat there ever so high on her head!"—which he evidently considered a sign of considerable distinction.

We were much amused with this old miner's candour. No doubt, having lived in the mountains all his life, he expected us to appear in silk gowns of bright colours, like the pictures of beautiful ladies on pin-boxes. Instead of this, we took the greatest trouble to procure sufficiently rough clothes for the life out here, and wear the same day after day.

The miners here are very simple in some ways, and are apt to take things in too literal a sense. They are very much down on ignorance of facts with which they are acquainted. For instance, I gave them some books which I thought would interest them; they were selected by a friend, and, needless to relate, were tales with a good moral tendency. One of the books was called, "The Californian Gold-Digger." A few days after their distribution, Frank, one of the miners, told me "The story was not true;" that the whole thing was impossible; that he had read it; that "no woman could wander in the woods with her child in a carriage for days together;" in the first place the carriage could not travel in the woods. In fact, he was prepared to argue that the greater part of the story was incorrect. No doubt he was right. Experienced in the life of the woods, the inaccuracies struck him, and in such a way that he doubted the whole of the book, and the author's ultimate design was lost.

In another book the word "salvation" was mentioned.

A miner asked Adela confidentially whether I belonged to the Salvation Army, as I had given him a book with the word in it. Alas! their utter ignorance and lack of religious teaching made me feel quite sad.

The two maids were sulky, so Adela and I had a day's washing, and after it was over were glad to see all the clothes clean and hanging up to dry; half an hour's washing, however, made my back and shoulders ache. For those who only know the smooth side of life and are dissatisfied, how excellent it would be if they were exiled even for a month, and deprived of most of the comforts of home life; on their return, how they would appreciate them!

In the afternoon one of the Indians who started with Algernon and N—— came galloping up to the "shack." We ran out to hear the news. Asked if he had a letter, he looked at us in silence, for an Indian is always dignified and reserved; but still he sat there, and I found, after waiting some time, that he had a haunch of venison fastened in a sack behind the saddle. We concluded this to be the reason of his visit, and quickly appropriated the venison. We had been without fresh meat for some days, so were glad of it. Afterwards we found this meat had been shot by some of the Indians. He had only come to have a look at us on the way down the trail, "white squaws" being still a curiosity in the Kootenay valley. Tom C—— said I was the first person he had met who had got something from an Indian for nothing! A few days afterwards I saw the same Indian again, and paid him for what I had so calmly taken.

Found the black horse to-day nearly strangled. He had contrived to tie up his legs in a manner worthy of Maskelyne and Cooke's best efforts; so much so, that in a few hours he would have died; I cut him loose. A clever cow pony will never come to grief with a lariat, and can generally unwind himself by going the reverse way. This was a tiresome, stupid animal all the time we had him. It is most dangerous—so far as the ponies are concerned —to place a knot at the end of a lariat, as in the event of a stampede the horse may hang himself by means of the knot, and starve to death. Instances, alas! are not uncommon of ponies having met this fate.

As I was painting this afternoon, one of the miners came with a message, and asked if he might see my sketches, as he had "never seen a picture painted with a brush." He looked with interest at several, and then said, "Well, I never thought as how one could do all these things with a brush and pencil. I thought as how all these things were done by machinery." This man had lived in the mountains for thirty-three years, and when I told him of the prices which were given for beautiful pictures, he seemed utterly astonished.

September 22*nd.*—The weather commences to feel wintry, and the nights are very cold; the wind blows through this wooden house, and there is a feeling of snow in the keen air. The hunters have returned this evening; both look tired, having had no sport. I copy from Algernon's diary an account of their week's expedition :—

THE CAMP AT SKOOKUM-CHUCK.

"We left with three Kootenays, all riding, and a pack-
"pony, to look for goat. The trail, after leaving the flat
"on the other side of Findlay Creek, was very rough, full
"of fallen timber, bogs, and nearly perpendicular bluffs.
"Our animals are excellent mountain ponies. We camped
"the first night about half-way to Skookum-chuck ('quick
"water'), at an old prospector's camp. No tent required,
"as the night was lovely. The ponies found plenty of
"grass as we hobbled them.

"Started at 5 A.M. A much worse trail; one of the
"Indians staked his pony, and had to leave him hobbled
"on the trail. Got to Skookum-chuck at 4 P.M.; went
"to look for deer.

"*Tuesday.*—This is a lovely creek and fine scenery.
"We went along the bank up-stream for about six hours,
"and camped at an old Indian camp—quite the most
"beautiful situation one could imagine. I wished to try
"for goat here, as there were heaps of fresh sign, but
"the Indians said there were none here now, and promised
"any number farther up the creek. N—— and I
"went up a goat-trail in the evening, and waited in hopes
"of catching one coming down from the range to drink,
"but had no luck.

"*Wednesday.*—Went further up the creek to the pro-
"mised 'happy hunting-grounds.' I climbed a nearly
"perpendicular mountain 3,000 or 4,000 feet, and when
"on top, saw only a succession of precipices, with no sign
"of goat. The Indian went as fast as he could, and had
"no knowledge of hunting—more of trying to run me out

"of sight; so I told him, 'Not my idea of hunting; no
"sign of goat.' This made Louis very sulky, and as they
"were utterly useless as hunters, we decided to return.

"*Friday.*—Started at dawn, after some trouble in
"catching Pongo, N——'s pony. The trail led first up a
"terribly steep zigzag for 2,000 or 3,000 feet; then a
"descent began through very thick scrub over our heads,
"through which we made our way as best we could, over
"endless 'windfalls' and rocks. By this time it was pour-
"ing with rain, and at intervals it changed to heavy sleet
"or snow, so that in a short time we had not a dry rag on
"us. After several hours of this work, the trail having
"quite given out, we scaled another mountain. Struck
"the trail near the top, and at last got well above the
"snow-line, making up our minds to camp in an old crater
"we found with a small lake in it—a most lovely spot.
"Just as we were getting down to the lake, Louis, who
"was a few yards ahead with the pack-pony, saw a small
"bear, and at once fired, without waiting for one of us.
"Needless to say, he missed, as most of the Indians are
"poor shots, especially at any running object. For any one
"who could shoot at all, it would have been an easy mark.
"After changing into some dry things, as it was freezing as
"hard as it could up here, I went out to prospect for goat,
"but with no better luck, beyond seeing some old tracks.

"*Saturday.*—An early start. The scenery when we rode
"on to the summit from our camping-ground was most
"magnificent. The Selkirks and Rockies, with their tops
"covered with snow, and with the rising sun shining on

" them, extended for hundreds of miles around us, for we
" were at a great height, and in a wonderfully clear atmo-
" sphere. A rough trail and steep. We reached the C——'s
" camp tired and hungry."

From the foregoing, one can see that many of the Indians at the present time will take sportsmen away from game, so anxious are they to keep it for themselves. Those districts where the Indians are great hunters are the worst places for white men to find sport.

September 25th.—I now resume my journal. The horses all stampeded during the night, though picketed with the greatest care; but the soil here holds picket-pins very badly. We thought a bear or wolf must have been the cause. We found it most annoying; all had to turn out to search for the missing horses. We walked in different directions, and for many hours; sometimes a burnt stump in the far distance seemed to shape itself to one's excited imagination into the form of one of the black ponies. We met the Indian pony staked at Skookum-chuck, looking well and fat; then we got on the trail of a lariat, and followed a long distance, only to find a black horse belonging to the upper camp. Starlight at last we found wandering alone, with his lariat broken, and saw other five ponies, but alas! none of them ours. The sun was hot, and walking through the long grass and windfalls was very fatiguing; at length we began to retrace our steps.

I was glad to meet Algernon with Adela's horse, on

which he had put a Californian saddle, and come to find me from the upper camp. I tried to ride sideways, but that did not do, so seated myself in the ordinary way. I suppose custom is everything, but I felt very little would send me flying—an inglorious voluntary. All the squaws "out West" ride across, and ride very well.

On reaching the upper camp, met Adela. She had found all the horses except one—the black one with a white blaze—our bane, and also not paid for! We spent the afternoon looking for him, without success.

September 26*th*.—Algernon was up early, and shot a grey wolf which was trying to play with the dogs; a huge brute it was, with a good coat, and not unlike an "Esqui" dog in colour. We had heard the wolves making a great noise for several nights, but did not think they would venture so near in the daytime. Algernon prepared the head for stuffing, and the skin was stretched to dry on the wall in the sun.

Adela and I searched for the lost pony. We feared he was stolen, or hung up somewhere in the way I have already described; if the latter, we felt no time was to be lost, so we searched all the woods round for him, but with no success.

We never saw or heard of him again.

CHAPTER XV.

IN SEARCH OF BETTER SPORT—LIFE AT FINDLAY
CREEK—GOOD-BYE—DAYS ON THE TRAIL.

"And so in mountain solitudes o'ertaken,
   As by some spell divine
Their cares drop from them, like the needles shaken
   From out the gusty pine."—*Bret Harte.*

Findlay Creek, September 27th.—Algernon and N—— said good-bye to Findlay Creek, having arranged to meet their hunters at Windermere. Tom C—— went also on his way to Calgary. Adela and I rode part of the way with them, and I felt rather depressed at being left behind, but Algernon thought I could not stand the rough work or walking.

Margeau, the half-breed, one of the best hunters in the Kootenay Valley, when they saw him three weeks ago, told them that last year he was out with two Austrians; they had seven pack ponies, and as far as he could see, one of the ponies carried a load of white pocket-handkerchiefs! the quantity of "kit" these men had seemed to amuse him very much.

Algernon and N—— have started off on this their third hunt with renewed hope and energy.

The house was very lonely to-night with all the men gone, and the stillness only broken by the dismal howling of the wolves. But though we hung up the carcase of the dead wolf as a bait, we did not get a shot, these animals being most wary.

Our days were mostly spent in riding about seeking for the missing horse, and in visiting the hydraulic. The weather was delightful, a hot sun with a light breeze off the mountains. We passed in our rides sometimes over flats covered with bunch grass, and here and there clumps of pine-trees, with high wooded hills on either side; now and then our ponies had to climb over windfalls or down the side of some steep rocky gulch.

I had my rifle hitched to my saddle, and felt happier with it there. We passed many elk-horns lying about, some of them large ones. The Indians seem to have cleared this part of the country of game; last year at their Christmas feast they had 800 deer; they kill them in season and out of season, which seems a great pity.

My pony "Baldie" and I have become good friends; he is a queer-looking creature, with a white blaze on his forehead and four white legs, but pretty tough and a good hack. If he is given an hour or two's rest with his saddle off (when he enjoys a good roll), he can canter along with me all day; he likes to drink at every creek he passes, and no amount of water seems to do him any harm.

October 2nd.—There is much sameness in our daily record. We eat, drink, and sleep; we would read books, but that our small library has become exhausted. No post, no church, no garden, and all the wool I was making stockings with is also finished.

The miners have almost got down to the bed-rock in the river; hard work; the men continually have to keep moving large stones and rocks which impede their progress, and when unable to do so, they have to blow them up with dynamite. The Chinamen who work here are miserable-looking specimens, and do all this labour, feeding almost entirely on rice; the horrible effects of opium-smoking are seen in their languidness and death-like pallor.

The difficulties connected with mining here are very great. Though the men have only been working a short time, the ditch which carries the water has broken incessantly; this is from no fault in construction, but because the banks in some places have not settled. All this delays the work, for when a break occurs the water must at once be turned off at the nearest gate to prevent further damage. The ditch carrying the water for this hydraulic comes a distance of five miles.

October 3rd.—Last night I felt somewhat alarmed, having heard Indians passing just before we went to bed. Here we are with only two English maids and a lad who had lately come from England. Adela (to prevent my being frightened) assured me that there were no Indians, that I was mistaken, in fact, that it was only the lad snoring, but this morning we saw two Indians coming down from the upper camp; they had passed during the night, driving some cattle with them; these were the sounds that had disturbed me.

The Indians do not sell their calves, but sell yearlings which have been on the range the better part of two summers; the meat of these is excellent; perhaps feeding on the bunch grass brings the animal to earlier maturity than with us. A two-year-old steer, which will weigh 500 lbs., can be bought for \$30 = £8, his value when killed being about 6 cents per lb., or about 3d. in our money.

We called the Indians, as I wanted to buy some of their ornaments, and when they rode up to the house, we gave them each some tobacco, and I purchased from them an embroidered fire-bag, with a fringe of mink tails, and a bead necklace strung on leather. The Indians spoke to each other all the time, and I heard one of them say in Chinook "that there were a lot of Clootchmans (women) about." Adela whispered, "Let them go, it's time they went away." I saw she was uneasy, and I was not sorry when they rode off.

Our life here is an entirely outdoor one, and the weather having been so fine for the last six weeks, has made the greatest difference in the pleasure of our visit.

Whilst sketching one day, Adela and I viewed two

partridges; the gun was two miles away at the shack, but she quickly jumped on one of the ponies, and returned with it. We were so pleased, and even thought of our possible dinner. Alas! there is many a slip 'twixt the cup and the lip. The too impulsive deerhound ran in too soon, spoilt our chance, and we saw our hoped-for dinner fly away. Partridges are scarce here, owing to the number of grey wolves, which prey upon them when no larger game is to be procured.

We have been expecting C——'s return for the last three days; the anxiety of being without men in the house we do not like; I have kept my little Colt's repeating rifle loaded in my room, and Adela has a pistol.

We had almost given up hopes of him when I heard a holloa, and we saw a cloud of dust coming up the trail, and in a short time he was with us. His pony was about "played out." I took charge of poor "Whitebait," watered him, took off his saddle and bridle, and turned him loose; no wonder he was tired, for he had come about 80 miles in two days.

Adela tells us to-night how pleased she was when our Indian visitors rode away the other day, as she recognised one of them as "Capla" as soon as she saw them, he being the Indian who shot two white men in the valley some time before. The story is as follows, but certainly there were extenuating circumstances:—

In some out-of-the-way place, Capla met two miners; he was starving, and asked for food; this they refused to give, and moreover told him that they would shoot him if he did not " clear out." He went, but waited until they gave him a chance, and then shot them both. A squaw of his own tribe informed the police, but there was not sufficient evidence to convict him, and he got off; he has been rather avoided by the settlers and miners since that time.

One day I said to Frank (one of the miners), " Don't you know any good stories to tell me ? "

" Well, I guess, a good many. In the year 1863, a lot
" of us were up in the Yellowstone Park, at a place they
" called the Big Gulch. Well, the party were attacked by
" Indians ; we were eighteen hunters, but we knew that the
" 300 Indians would wipe us all out if they got the chance ;
" having a good quantity of ammunition, we were able to
" hold our own. One of the hunters had an Indian wife ;
" she fought for us against her people, killing seven Indians
" to her own rifle, and when the bullets were nearly all
" used up, she made more under a heavy fire. Ah ! she
" was a good woman for fighting ; we repulsed the attack
" after many hours.

" Yes, I could tell you many stories of things I've seen myself :—

" On the Mississippi one time, when the miners were
" away from camp, the Indians came down, cleared the
" camp of all that there was to carry away ; one person
" was in it, a white woman, the wife of one of rhe men ;
" her they knocked on the head and scalped, leaving her
" for dead. In the evening, however, when the miners
" returned, they found she was not dead but scalped, and

" what was worse, the scalp carried off, and irretrievably
" gone!"

" Did she live?" I asked.

" Oh, yes, she lived. She was ill all winter, but the
" boys made a sort of plaster of canvas and balsam they got
" off the trees, and put her head into a case of this, and
" when she got well they got her a wig. We were soon
" even with them; we killed eighteen Indians that night,
" and put their heads in a row close to where the steamer
" passed. Some fresh comers on board were shocked at
" the sight, called us cruel: we were armed, and forced them
" to leave the steamer, and come with us to our camp,
" where they saw the scalped woman. They did not call
" us cruel then!"

These pioneering days must have been troublesome and rough; although things are changed for the better now, so lately as five years ago our host found three dead men on the trail as he was coming up to Findlay Creek from Golden.

The Prairie Indians in the North-West Territory do not take to industrial pursuits like those in British Columbia, and for this reason, that while the former have Government grants and rations, the latter have none; therefore they like farming, fishing, lumbering, and such work, while the Prairie Indians, having no incentive to work, hunt, and this is their sole occupation. The system of reservations is just and right. They provide a settled home to those Indians who would otherwise be without land of their own; but education for the rising generation would be decidedly more advantageous than the system of rations, which only tends to pauperize them, while many of the poor Indians, being completely in the power of the agents who distribute the rations, are robbed by them in the most disgraceful manner.

In Canada the Indians are in undisputed possession of their reserves, and long may it be so, until time and the march of civilisation transform them into a useful population.

October 15*th.*—Lovely weather, with brilliant sunshine. Had we been in a log-house we should have felt perfectly warm; but it got bitterly cold at night in the "shack." When I opened my little window in the early morning, the temperature was the same outside and in; the water was frozen in my basin, and my sponge like a rock. Fortunately I have warm clothes—one requires them—and also I have a large indiarubber water-bag which is almost a necessity when travelling in out-of-the-way places, which I put into my bed at night, and is a great comfort. We have nailed woollen shawls up to keep off the draughts, as we were all beginning to suffer from the effects of them. A log-house is usually built by squaring the logs, and notching them where they cross at the corners, so that they fit closely together, the notches also binding the building firmly; the roof is also made of logs resting on a strong roof-tree, and covered with a foot of earth. If it be wished to make the house extra warm, the chinks between the logs are filled with moss.

A shack is built by nailing boards upright to a frame the size of the intended house; the roof is also of boards roughly nailed on, and the whole construction often leaks like a sieve.

A passing Indian promised to deliver a letter to Algernon. Having been paid, he started, after a long and animated conversation chiefly carried on by signs, during which he repeatedly nodded his head, and I fondly imagined understood. I enclosed my letter to Captain Armstrong, who, I knew, would send it to Algernon where he is hunting on Horse-thief Creek. (I may mention that the Indian did not fully understand me. He thought he had to find Algernon, and never went to Captain Armstrong. He followed the former's trail for three days, and then, finding it led over a small glacier, and a storm coming on, he, as the miners say, made tracks for home. As he had had a three days' ride for his two dollars, he was not overpaid, although unsuccessful in his mission.)

The stage waggon, with four very hard-worked-looking ponies, came up this afternoon. The driver told us that Capla, the Indian I mentioned before, "held up" a man yesterday and took $16 from him. To hold a man up in North-West parlance means to threaten to shoot him if he does not hold his hands up over his head. The man seemed frightened, and after being robbed offered Capla his watch, which was promptly thrown back in his face. We travel over the same trail to-morrow and next day, but the driver has his revolver, and I decided to hitch my rifle on to my saddle.

Said good-bye to Findlay Creek. I was sorry to leave the C——s behind (they are going to move to the log camp farther up the valley), but glad to leave the place, as the cold was intense, being below zero. I preferred to ride all the way, as the jolting and discomfort of driving over a rough trail is more easily imagined than described. We all breakfasted in our fur cloaks, but the bright sunshine soon made us feel warmer.

The stage waggon came to the door at 8 A.M. The baggage was quickly packed; the C——s sent all their heavy things, as this was the last chance of their having them conveyed by steamer on the Columbia this year, as the river was beginning to freeze up. Then Adela's two maids, who looked upon their journey as a very important one, were seated, and lastly Percy D——, who seems to have had enough gold-mining for the present, one half-day's hard work at the hydraulic having damped his youthful ardour.

Fresh snow lies on the mountains everywhere; white hoar-frost has covered the trees, the leaves, and the grass, and the ground crackles under the weight of the ponies and waggon. So cold is it that I am glad to fasten my big cloak round me as I ride along.

Findlay Creek looked its best as we were leaving; the mountains covered with snow, the foreground of larch and dark green stone-pine standing out sharply in the clear atmosphere of a winter day. The trail about 150 feet above the creek did not daunt the Jehu of the waggon, who, by many imprecations, threats, and a free use of the whip, urged the ponies into a hand-gallop, and, with only sufficient room for the waggon to pass, they made the best pace they could over a very bad road. Custom certainly makes a difference to every one; indeed, I am not at all sure that habit is not often mistaken for courage. A man accustomed to horses is not afraid of them, neither is a sailor afraid in a boat, but a tailor or a landsman might in their places be wrongly mistaken for a coward.

CHAPTER XVI.

BREWER'S " STOPPING-HOUSE "—HOT SPRINGS—INDIAN
WOMEN—FROM WINDERMERE TO GOLDEN CITY.

" From toil he wins his spirits light,
From busy day the peaceful night;
Rich, from the very want of wealth,
In heaven's best treasures, peace and health."—*Grey*.

AFTER an eight hours' ride Mrs Brewer, the wife of the proprietor of the " stopping-house " at Hot Springs, greets me at her door with " Oh ! you've come, have you ? I was expecting you."

Adela's two maids and Percy D—— arrive ten minutes later in the waggon. It amuses me to notice that the maids have donned a quantity of tawdry jewellery during their drive; this seems to impress Mrs. Brewer, who receives them as visitors of much greater distinction than myself. We follow her into the kitchen, and not having had anything to eat since 7 A.M., I ask for a cup of tea. She says nothing, but begins an impromptu toilet, first brushing and replaiting her hair, then by placing a tin basin on the stove she contrives to get the chill off the water, and with the aid of some yellow soap produces a most excellent polish on her good-humoured face; she then suddenly appears in a clean gown, fastening with the aid of a large brass pin, a coloured kerchief round her neck, and while donning these garments keeps up a running conversation with us, the principal subject of it being complaints of how Brewer's manners have fallen off since he came to this country! Mrs. Brewer, though Irish, is a good type of a " western woman," for she does the whole work of the stopping-house," having to get through all the cleaning and cooking, besides the waiting on fourteen or fifteen people at their meals three times a day. I am so much amused with her and her conversation that I forget all about my tea, and having been told there are sulphur springs near here, am just starting out to find them, when I am recalled by Mrs. Brewer's lusty voice, " It is only at " this first tea that stewed cabbage and hashed turnips are " provided," so I gladly sit down at once to revel in these delicacies of civilisation! The meat, however, is very tough, rather makes me fancy I am eating the sole of my shoe ; but there are excellent rolls, potatoes, and molasses.

Brewer is a hard-working man, and in spite of his wife's complaints of the effects of British Columbia on his manners, I find they are still much better than her own. Every picture has its pathetic side. This couple have been married thirteen years and have one small child, poor little fellow! when only eight months old he fell into the fire, and half his face was dreadfully burnt; the hard-working mother stopped to tell me all about the accident, and of how unhappy they both were when they thought they would lose him. In their love the disfigurements of his little face are forgotten! There are no fewer than sixteen cats under the stove; the little burnt child sits and hugs the kittens in his arms, until one wonders they are not squeezed to death. This army of cats is required to keep the mountain rats in check; they are very destructive and will ruin a saddle in a few hours, and have a curious habit of carrying any shining object to their holes; they will also empty a sack of grain in an incredibly short time.

Brewer came to talk to me after tea; he asked me if I should like to see his gold nuggets, and having replied in the affirmative, he returned presently with several small canvas bags full of them; the value of the gold he said was about £300. Here, with all sorts of people coming and going, he seemed to have no anxiety about the safety of his treasure. This speaks well for the country.

I must also mention that during the whole time of our visit in the mountains, though we kept all the saddles, bridles, and lariats under the verandah by the front door, nothing was ever lost or missing.

I started for the Hot Springs after tea. A climb over a steep trail of nearly a mile brought me to the first basin, the water of which is perfectly hot and very clear; it is eight or nine feet long, about two feet deep and four feet wide; the overflow leaves a curious rocky-looking deposit, and in the crevices of the sandstone below quantities of maiden-hair fern grow. It is curious to see such delicate ferns growing here where the temperature is so low at night; but if one feels the ground, it proves quite warm, and must have, therefore, the same effect as a hot-bed.

On going a couple of hundred yards further and making a steep descent, I found myself by the side of a mountain stream. Another large basin had been formed here, and into it the clear water comes bubbling up boiling hot, looking like champagne, while by the side of it runs the icy cold water of the mountain stream. I felt much tempted to have a bathe, but just as I had made up my mind to do so two miners appeared on the scene.

October 16*th.*—The mail waggon did not start till 12.30, and we had a shorter distance to go to-day, so I amuse myself wandering about. The morning was very cold and sunless, but fortunately the snow kept off. The trail seemed quite lively with passers-by; first come three bullock teams, hauling heavy loads of lumber; the great creatures move slowly but do ten miles a day, oxen taking much longer to feed than horses. Then pass three squaws, with ten ponies, evidently following the men who went up yesterday evening, on their way to hunt. The women ride astride their saddles, and do not seem to mind what load their ponies carry. One squaw has two boys on the pony with her, another carries in the hood of her blanket a crying *papoose*, while the third conveys a cat in the same way. The children seem much frightened when I go to speak to them, evidently not being used to "white" people. I make them understand by signs that I wish to purchase one of their "quirts" (riding-whips); they seem amused, and I secure one for $1. It consists of a short wooden handle, painted red and ornamented with brass nails, having at one end a loop of coloured cloth for the wrist and at the other end two leather thongs, which form a lash about two feet long.

At last the time came to start; the four ponies were caught, and harnessed to the waggon. I saddled up Baldy, and said good-bye to Mrs. Brewer, who regretted that she had not had more time to talk to me and to the two maids!

Shortly before we left, a waggon arrived from Canal Flat with two poor men in it very ill with mountain fever; they asked for beef tea; stewed beef was offered to them instead. Fortunately I had a sausage of Brand's beef tea, and was very glad to give them some of it. (For the next three days they happened to travel with me, and I was able to doctor them with chlorodyne, and other things, which I think saved their lives; they had no one else to look after them.)

I kept as near the waggon as I could, as there had been a scare about the Indians the day before. At one place we heard some shouting, but found it was only some Indians bringing a band of horses down the trail. They generally on good ground go at full gallop and seldom lose a pony, as they are accustomed to be driven in this way. From the time they are small foals they follow their mothers, and instances have been known of their going forty to sixty miles when only a week old. In this way they become tractable before they are broken. All the time we were in British Columbia, we never saw a lame or broken-kneed pony, although taken very long journeys. Percy D—— got the loan of a pony, and therefore I had a companion for the remainder of my ride to Windermere, of which I was glad, as to ride with a waggon is to go at a very tiresome pace.

We cantered along leaving the stage far behind, and just as it was getting dark, reached the wooden house near the Columbia Lake, which is designated the "Windermere Hotel." Imagine my pleasure; the first person who greeted me was Algernon; he and N—— had both come in from the mountains two hours before, and were greatly astonished to see me, thinking I had left Findlay Creek some time ago. They looked tired and unkempt, having been for twenty-four hours without food.

Everything was beautifully clean, and we enjoyed a most excellent tea, the only drawback to our repose and comfort being the "Saloon" or "Bar." After we had gone to bed, there was too much noise to allow us to sleep, and the drunken orgie ended in what they call a "Bull's Ball" in this country. A fiddler arrived, about thirty men danced together, and the shuffling of feet and the talking and the laughing, and the reek of bad tobacco, disturbed us until an early hour the next morning.

Algernon is wakened by N—— at 4 A.M., and on going out to the stables they find the white pony and another, belonging to the manager of the hotel, gone; but after an hour's search, they are both recovered. One of the drunken heroes of the night's merry-making let them out of the stables. At first we heard that they were stolen, and Algernon at once equipped himself to go after the thief. I was so glad that this was not necessary, as besides the risks, had he ridden in the opposite direction, we should have missed the steamer, the last one down the Columbia this year, and I heard that the 150 miles' ride to Golden was over a very bad trail.

Algernon saddled the ponies and we started for the ten-mile ride down the trail to the steamer. The weather looked threatening, but fortunately held up until we were quite near the end of our ride. Three waggons with passengers of all sorts followed us. The Government have been improving the trail, which is now much better than it was last year. At length we reached the boat, and were welcomed by Captain Armstrong, and as there is no cabin on the *Marion*, we were glad to avail ourselves of his kind offer of tea in the warehouse, where there is a cooking-stove, used to prepare food for some men whom he has working above here to improve the channel of the river. At first the prospects of our journey looked gloomy enough. There was no possible room for the ponies on board, and it seemed as likely as not that we should have to ride them ourselves all the way to Golden. Fortunately, as the boat was about to start, a man was found who was willing to take them down for us for the sum of $12.

There was a board roof or hurricane deck, with canvas

hangings at the sides, which afforded some shelter against the rain, which came down in torrents. The passengers sat shivering round the funnel of the steamer, while the poor sick men were stretched out on blankets amidships. The larger steamer *The Duchess* no longer runs on the river, as she draws too much water. The *Marion*, therefore, a much smaller boat, has taken her place, which the men say could float in a heavy dew! When full of cargo and passengers, she draws little more than a foot of water.

The day improved as we ran down the river, and the wheel-house where Captain Armstrong allowed us to sit was certainly the most comfortable place in the boat, and from it we had beautiful views of the river as we steamed along. The heavy mist rose slowly off the mountains on either side of the valley, and let us see the hills, quite white with snow.

Bump! bump! bump! and we were aground upon a sand-bank. After much patient work with poles, and having made a hawser fast to a tree on the bank, which all the men on board hauled at with a will, the *Marion* was floated again. This happened several times, and rendered our progress rather slow.

At one place, as we drew near the bank to "wood up," —as taking on board wood for the engines is called,—Algernon sees Moulson, a miner and hunter whom we saw on our way up. He tells us that the Shushwap Indians have had good hunting in the neighbourhood, so Algernon decides to remain for a week and have a hunt with him. We hastily collect his blankets, rifle, cartridges, and kit-bag, have only just time to say good-bye before the steamer starts, and we leave them standing on the bank. N—— has had enough of it, he says; and certainly it must be very cold work camping out at night, with the thermometer below zero.

The storm which was so severe in the mountains a few days ago is over, and after the first fall of snow there is often a good chance of getting bear, before they finally settle down in their winter quarters.

I much wished to stay with Algernon, but N—— and Captain Armstrong advised me strongly against doing so, both on account of the cold and also because a third person's presence might diminish the chances of sport; and further, they will need a pack-pony, and they hope to get ours on the way to Golden.

N—— goes to Mitford *en route* for England at once, while I am bound for Banff Hotel as the nearest point where I can wait for Algernon. Meantime, as we steam along, the amusement of firing at ducks and geese with a rifle is diverting; but as the birds get alarmed the moment they hear the boat coming, we put down the rifles. Then, bad luck! from a bed of rushes up rise three large geese.

All the lakes which lie along the Columbia valley are covered with wild-fowl at the present time; besides wild swan, there are geese, ducks, herons, bitterns, grebes, pelicans, and many other varieties in abundance. We hear the weird cries of many of these birds towards evening, and it becomes too dark at 6 o'clock to proceed further.

The steamboat is moored near the bank, by a log-house

owned by a man called "Dutch Pete"—not an uncommon name in the Columbia valley, for we have already heard of "Shushwap Pete" and "Kootenay Pete."

Our landlord looks exactly as if he had tumbled out of one of Teniers' pictures; he is rather stout, with fair hair, has a Dutch-looking face, wears a round-brimmed hat, and the inevitable pipe is always in his mouth; and though apparently rather overwhelmed by such a sudden invasion, he soon rises to the emergency. He has to prepare supper for twelve hungry people. The log-house is divided into three rooms; in one of them the sick men are lodged; in the centre room, which is provided with a good wooden table and long benches, we are all glad to sit down and wait for supper.

There are three women on the steamer besides myself; they have the third room allotted to them, while Captain Armstrong kindly gives me the wheel-house on the steamer as my sleeping-place. It has the merit of being quiet, and though it is tiny, I have it all to myself; so with my warm blankets and fur rugs, I shall be fairly comfortable, and able to defy the weather. The night air is exceedingly cold, and the evening almost as light as day now the moon is up, and thousands of stars are visible.

We are all very hungry, and glad when, after a great deal of shuffling, whispering, and preparation, supper is at last ready; and really excellent it is for such a place, for we have beefsteaks (where from?) and baked potatoes, hot rolls and tea, with good salt butter. I sit near Captain

P

Armstrong; opposite to me is a female passenger, returning from Windermere. She wears upon her head a thing they please to call a "Fascinator." It fascinates me, but not in the way its owner would wish; for as I look at this comical brown woollen head-dress trimmed with beads, it makes me smile, in spite of my efforts not to do so. I am asked to explain the reason of my amusement by N—— and Captain Armstrong, but of course I cannot.

Some one to-morrow will mourn the loss of these beef-steaks which we have so much appreciated this evening, because they were put in a "*cache*" * by a boatman who went up the river yesterday, for food on the way down. No ill-feeling seems to result from thus taking possession of the property of another; that it was required to feed hungry people seems sufficient excuse.

This stopping-house is what I expected, but the English maids, who have been rendered perfectly unbearable by the attentions they have received during their exit from British Columbia, complain bitterly of their discomforts, and of the cold.

In order to be a good traveller, one must always be prepared to accept the inevitable, and I am sure this rule would also apply well to all travellers on life's journey. These months in the Rocky Mountains have taught me a great deal in that way. When I see these poor sick men enduring all this cold and fatigue uncomplainingly, I thank God that we are all well after our wanderings.

* Hiding-place.

Fortunately I have tinned soup, quinine, and other things with me, so that I am able to look after the invalids.

Nature is very beautiful and perfect in her dispositions; in most places in these mountains grows the "mahonia" or Oregon grape; also the white sage. The root and berries of the mahonia infused as a strong tea, or the leaves of the sage treated in the same way, as the settlers say, "breaks the fever," or in other words, is an excellent remedy. With considerable trouble, we had collected some of the roots of the mahonia, and were preparing it in the above manner, but the untiring "Dutch Pete," who desired to put everything in order, threw it away when we left the room for a few minutes!

Life is a struggle, a survival of the fittest; but this is surely a sorry place for invalids, but in spite of many drawbacks, the patients are improving; moving homewards possibly cheers them.

Ere long I return to my little wheel-house on the steamer, and after wrapping myself up in the warmest possible way, soon fall asleep. Sounds of wood-chopping and of engine fires being lighted are the first I hear in the morning; then the more welcome call to breakfast; after that we soon start again.

I left in the care of "Dutch Pete" two extra plaids, which he promised to deliver to Algernon, the weather being so extremely cold that I feared he had not taken sufficiently warm things with him; these never reached him. All these hunting expeditions are a great anxiety to me.

On the Cars.—Our steamboat *Marion* reached the wharf half-a-mile from Golden, at three o'clock. At six o'clock, N—— and I stepped into the cars, and were again surrounded by comforts of all kinds.

Snow all round us, and by moonlight we have occasional glimpses of the wondrous scenery through which we are passing. Before Banff is reached, the snow has become quite deep. All looks horridly wintry, the severe cold having come rather suddenly; however, we have little to complain about, this having been one of the finest autumns on record in the North-West.

October 19th.—Wish N—— good-bye; step out on the snowy platform 3 A.M. A quick drive takes me to the Banff Springs Hotel.

Nothing to do but rest and get my luggage unpacked. The hot air after the freshness in the mountains is to me intolerable; I am obliged to sleep with all my windows open.

Find some Canadians whom we met at Vancouver; one of them plays most charmingly. There is a new Steinway grand piano in the hotel. As I listen to Chopin's Nocturnes and Brahm's Hungarian dances, I close my eyes and think of all we have seen and done, with a feeling of security and rest which is delightful, although I thoroughly enjoyed the free life in the mountains.

The season at Banff is over; all the large rooms are

closed. Still by every train one or two travellers arrive, either on their way to the coast or homeward bound. The hotel, however, though half empty, is not devoid of some romance. " 'Tis love, 'tis love that makes the world go round." A bridal pair are in the house, having been married in the small English church here last Tuesday.

October 21st.—Nice simple service in the English church; there are also Presbyterian and Methodist services held here every Sunday.

October 25th.—More snow. It is coming down in powdery flakes to-day. Had a lovely drive in a sledge; with the bells it sounded cheerful. All carts and waggons are now on runners, and the river is frozen, which gives the place quite an unfamiliar look.

The horrors of being frost-bitten are not an uncommon experience here, but the speedy application of snow to the affected parts, or, in the case of the hands and feet, plunging them into cold water and keeping them there while the thawing process is going on, prevents much harm being done except in very aggravated cases.

Played a rubber of whist this evening, and discovered that in "American whist" honours do not count, and short whist is seven, not five, as with us.

CHAPTER XVII.

NOTES ABOUT EARLY FRENCH SETTLERS—HUNTING IN THE MOUNTAINS.

" What man would read and read the self-same faces,
  And like the marbles which the windmill grinds,
  Rub smooth for ever with the same smooth minds,
  This year retracing last year's, every year's dull traces,
  When there are woods and un-man-stifled places?"--*Lowell*.

Banff Springs Hotel, Rocky Mountains.—Some of the early Canadian histories are very interesting; among others, 'The Old Régime in Canada,' by Parkman, and extracts from old French letters given in this work are specially quaint and curious.

Early in the 17th century we find the following entries relating to the *noblesse* who had emigrated to Canada during the reign of Louis XIV.:—

"The *gentilhomme* had no vocation for emigrating. He
" liked the army; he liked the Court. If he could not be
" of it, it was something to live in its shadow. The life of
" a backwoods settler had no charm for him; he was not
" used to labour, and he could not trade without being
" liable to forfeit his nobility."

"When Talon came to Canada, there were but four

"noble families in the Colony. Where, then, could be
"found the material for a Canadian *noblesse?* First, in
"the regiment Carignan Salieres, sent from France by
"command of Louis XIV., for the assistance of his Cana-
"dian colony. Two hundred of them landed at Quebec,
"1665. Most of the officers of the expedition were *gentils-*
"*hommes.* Secondly, in the issue of patents of nobility.
"Stracy asked for four such patents; Talon for five more.
"Money smoothed the path to advancement.*

"Jacques le Ber, the merchant who had long kept a
"shop at Montreal, got himself made a gentleman for
"6,000 livres."† They did not, however, make much
progress or continue to flourish, as seen by the following
extracts from letters:—

"Many of our *gentilshommes officiers* and other owners of
"seignories lead what in France is called the life of a
"country gentleman, and spend most of their time in
"hunting or fishing. As their requirements in food and
"clothing are greater than those of the simple habitants,
"and as they do not devote themselves to the improving of
"their land, they mix themselves up in trade, run into debt
"on all hands, incite their young habitants to range the
"woods, and send their own children there to trade for furs
"in the Indian villages and in the depth of the forest, in
"spite of the prohibition of His Majesty. Yet with all
"this they are in miserable poverty." ‡

* Talon's 'Memoire sur l'Etat présent du Canada,' 1667.
† *Ex* 'Vie de Mademoiselle le Ber,' 325.
‡ "Lettre de Duchesneau au Ministre," 10 Novembre, 1679.

"It is pitiful to see their children, of whom they have great
"numbers, passing all the summer with nothing on them
"but a shirt, and their wives and daughters working in the
"fields." *

"We must give them some corn at once, or they will
"starve." †

"Above all things, monseigneur, permit me to say that
"the nobles of this new country are everything that is most
"beggarly, and that to increase the number is to increase
"the number of do-nothings. A new country requires
"hard workers, who will handle the axe or mattock."

"The sons of our councillors are no more industrious
"than the nobles, and their only resource is to take to the
"woods, trade a little with the Indians, and for the most
"part, fall into the disorders of which I have had the
"honour to inform you. I shall use all possible means to
"induce them to engage in regular commerce; but as our
"nobles and councillors are all very poor and weighed
"down with debt, they could not get credit for a single
"crown-piece." ‡

Louis XIV., dispenser of charity, came to the rescue.
He granted an alms of 100 crowns to each family, coupled
with a warning to the recipients of his bounty that "their
misery proceeds from their ambition to live as persons of
quality and without labour." §

* "Lettre de Champigny au Ministre," 26 Août, 1687.
† *Ibid.*, 6 Novembre, 1687.
‡ Abstract of Denonville's letters and of minister's answers, N.Y. Colonial Documents, IX. 317, 318.
§ 'Old Régime in Canada,' Parkman.

TRADE AS THE ONLY FIELD OF ACTION.

"Nobles in Canada were also permitted to trade even at "retail, without derogating from their rank." *

"Time and hardships, however, seem to have made "later on pioneers of these same men, who are spoken of "thus contemptuously;" and still writing of the early settler, the letter continues, "and it is no matter of "wonder that he threw himself into the only field of action "which in time of peace was open to him. It was trade, "but trade seasoned by adventure and ennobled by danger; "defiant of edict and ordinance, outlawed, conducted in "arms among forests and savages." In short, it was the western fur trade. The tyro was likely to fail in it at first, but time and experience formed him to the work.

"On the Great Lakes, in the wastes of the North-West, "on the Mississippi and the plains beyond, we find the "roving *gentilhomme*, chief of a gang of bushrangers often "his own habitants; sometimes proscribed by the Govern- "ment, sometimes leagued in contraband traffic with its "highest officials, a hardy vidette of civilization, tracing "unknown streams, piercing unknown forests, trading, "fighting, negotiating, and building forts. Again we find "him on the shores of Acadia or Maine, surrounded by "Indian retainers, a menace and a terror to the neigh- "bouring English colonist.

"Saint Custin, Du Slent La Darantaye, La Salle, La "Motte-Cadillac, Iberville, Bienville, La Verendrye, are "names that stand conspicuous on the pages of half-savage

* "Lettre de Meules au Ministre," 1685.

"romance, that refreshes the hard and practical annals of
" American colonisation. It was they and such as they
" who discovered the Ohio, explored the Mississippi to its
" mouth, discovered the Rocky Mountains, and founded
" Detroit, St. Louis, and New Orleans.

"In the summer of 1648 was held at the mission
" station of Sillery, a temperance meeting, the first in all
" probability on this continent. In the eyes of the
" missionaries, brandy was a fiend with all crimes and
" miseries in its train. The Jesuits of that day went with
" a high hand into the work of reform, and it fared ill
" with any found selling brandy to the Indians." *

Now after more than two hundred years have passed, under a different government, and a new régime, with the country civilized, it is somewhat curious to find the same law still existing over the North-West Territory. Any one at the present time found selling spirits to Indians is liable to be heavily fined, and there exists a prohibition against any spirituous liquors being brought into the country without a permit. In spite of these restrictions however, I am sorry to say a great deal of drinking goes on, and now most of the large hotels have got a permit, which makes this law in reality a farce.

October 28th.—Algernon returned at 12 P.M., having had bad sport. In his own words follow the accounts of his two hunting expeditions.

"*Windermere, October 4th.*—We are still here, having

* 'Old Régime in Canada,' Parkman.

"waited for Margeau. Having nothing else to do, we
paddled across the lake at daybreak, and spent most of
the day cruising through the woods looking for deer, but
saw none. Margeau arrived this evening, so we are to
start to-morrow.

"*October 5th.*—Up at break of day; packed our kit.
Baptiste and Prevost arrived at 9.30, when we packed
two ponies and started for Horse-Thief Creek. Margeau's
wife, a Kootenay, and his daughter, a pretty girl and
capital rider, came up with us, as they wanted to gather
blueberries to preserve for the winter, and, like all people
of Indian blood, love to get into the woods. When we
came to the crossing at Horse-Thief Creek it was bank-
full, and as we did not want to wet our packs, we took
them off the ponies and carried them over a fallen tree
which lay across the creek, making the ponies half wade,
half swim over. Margeau's girl rode her pony, though it
was swimming when in the middle of the creek. If it
had been carried off its legs, the girl would have had a
bad time, for the creek was flooded with glacier water.

"We camped as soon as everything had crossed, and
hobbled the ponies; the feed was poor, the fire having
run through the woods here. We drove them a little
way from the creek, and, having put a bell on my pony
and Margeau's, we left them to shift for themselves.

"*October 6th.*—Broke up camp at daybreak. Had some
trouble in finding the ponies. After going up the trail

"about six miles, we camped, and after watering the ponies
"and getting some dinner, went to look for bear. We saw
"some fresh tracks, but that was all. This place is where
"the sheriff caught the horse-thieves after whom the
"creek is named. They had camped here, and only one of
"them was in camp when the sheriff came on him; the
"other two were hunting, and were of course 'held up' as
"they were returning, suspecting nothing. Judging from
"the lot of beaver dams here, the number of camps and
"the amount of work they have done, there must be about
"thirty or forty beaver. I regretted much I had not
"brought up some traps, and should certainly have done
"so if I had known the country better.

"Baptiste's wife and daughter were delighted with the
"profusion of berries growing about here, and by evening
"had filled everything which they had with them in the
"way of bags; so they returned home next morning.

"*October 7th.*—We came up about six miles; some of
"the trail pretty rough. Camped on a flat by the creek,
"and hunted for bear with no better success, although
"there were plenty of fresh tracks.

"Bears are most shy, and have wonderful noses, though
"their sight is poor, and in the mountains, where the wind
"hardly ever blows fair in one direction for half an hour,
"they have every chance in their favour of scenting the
"hunter before they are themselves seen.

"*October 8th.*—Started at break of day. The trail ended
"here, so we had to take through the woods as best we

" could. We had some tremendous climbing through heavy
" timber up one of the steepest mountains I could well
" imagine. The ponies were all good at the work and in
" hard condition, so that, with the exception of having to
" re-pack them once or twice when they shifted their loads
" by brushing against trees, we got on very well, and
" about 3 o'clock reached our intended camping-ground,
" just on the edge of the timber-line, a few hundred feet
" from the top of the range.

" Some Kootenays had camped here in the summer.
" There was first-rate water, wood, and plenty of excellent
" grass, so we and the ponies were all suited; the latter
" were soon hobbled and feeding up to their knees in grass.
" Our tents were pitched, and the rest of the evening spent
" in making the camp comfortable, and mending moccasins.

" *October 9th.*—We all started from camp together, spying
" the ground carefully when we reached the 'divide,' but
" saw nothing for a long time. At last Baptiste, who
" was ahead a few yards, came suddenly upon a goat. I
" just had a snap-shot as he bolted round some rocks, and
" missed him clean—bad luck! It was a great mistake and
" very much against my wish that we all kept together.
" Two people are quite enough, particularly where there are
" so many loose rocks, which one careless step may set
" rolling; added to which, four people cannot help making
" far too much noise to get near game on this open ground,
" where sound carries so easily.

" *October 10th.*—We again started from camp together,

"but after we had got a little beyond the divide above the
"camp, N—— and his man stopped. Baptiste and I went
"on over another ridge, then down into a deep valley, where
"we found fresh tracks, which we followed nearly down to
"the creek in the bottom, then up again and along the
"side of the mountain, over some very queer ground for
"climbing. At last we saw an old buck feeding, and, after
"a long stalk—for he was suspicious, and in a position to
"command a good view of most of the ground, and the
"wind as usual was very shifty—I was just getting into
"position for a shot when he bolted, and though I fired I
"did not get him.

"We saw three or four goats lying high up on the range
"on the opposite side of the valley we were in, but we had
"no blankets nor food, so had to leave them in peace, and
"got back to camp very late, rather tired and disappointed.
"We found N—— had prepared us an excellent supper,
"and had made his first attempt at baking, which was a
"great success.

"*October* 11*th*.—Woke up to find the tent weighed down
"with a load of snow; the ponies had worked their way
"nearly to the divide above the camp the night before, but
"the snow had driven them down far below us. We soon
"caught them and drove them up to camp, picketed them,
"and after breakfast loaded up the pack-ponies, and
"started over the range, a very rough trail, not improved
"by the wet snow.

"We crossed the first divide, and descended into the

A NARROW ESCAPE.

" valley beyond; the wet snow had made the going very
" bad, and when we left the high ground the ponies were at
" times nearly up to their hocks in mud. The next divide
" we had to cross was barred by a small glacier; the old
" snow was all gone, and nothing but 'glare' ice, with fresh
" loose snow, was left upon which to cross. Baptiste said
" he would try with a pack-pony first; so we chose what
" looked the best line, and he started, leading the pony by
" the lariat. They got half across the ice when the pony
" slipped, got frightened, lost its footing, and slid down the
" steep incline on its side at a great pace, Baptiste holding
" on by the lariat, and following in the same way. The
" pony spun round and round with the pace it was going,
" but the pack stopped him from rolling over on his back. I
" thought some one would be hurt, but at last they brought
" up in some snow, and were none the worse. It took a
" great deal of persuasion to get the pony to stand up again,
" as it was well scared; we ultimately got it and all the
" others over this place, and down some very bad rocks on
" the other side the divide; nothing but a goat or a good
" mountain pony would have got over this place; it is won-
" derful how they get about with a heavy pack or still
" heavier man on their backs.

" About 4.30 in the afternoon, we reached the creek we
" meant to camp on; excellent water, wood, and lots of
" grass again, added to which it looked good goat country.
" We turned the ponies loose after hobbling them, and had
" the tents up and dinner cooking; the glasses were got
" out, and with them we at once got a sight of three or

"four goats feeding nearly on the top of the mountain
" facing our camp.

"It was too late to go after them to-night, so we passed
" the time cutting a good supply of wood, but making as
" little noise as possible in doing so, as sound carries
" wonderfully on this high ground.

"*October* 12*th*.—We started directly it was light for the
" goats we had seen last night, but when we got high up,
" the wind kept shifting so much that, after waiting for
" some hours in hopes of its becoming settled, we decided
" to return, and wait for a better chance next day. The
" goats were still in the place we had seen them in the
" night before. By the time we got to camp, it looked
" as if we were in for a heavy storm.

"*October* 13*th*.—We found there had been a fall of snow
" in the night, but it stopped by daylight, and we started up
" to where we had seen the goats; we found by their tracks
" that they had moved, owing to the rough night. N——
" and Baptiste started after them; Prevost and I hunted
" along the ridge to the south-east, but saw neither goat nor
" tracks. The going was bad and in places dangerous, as
" the steep hill-sides had frozen in the early part of the
" night, and the snow prevented us seeing what we were
" treading on. I slipped in one bad place, and know I
" shall feel the strain I gave my side for some time.

"*October* 14*th*.—A really heavy snow-storm began after
" dark last night; this morning it is still snowing as it only

" can snow in these mountains; the air is full of driving
" powdery flakes, and the clouds, when one catches a sight
" of them, look as if there were plenty more to come. The
" thermometer has gone a good many degrees below zero,
" and as hunting is impossible, there is nothing to do
" but to drive the ponies up from below camp, as they
" seem inclined to work towards the Columbia, and then
" spend the day in camp.

" *October* 16*th*.—Our food was now about finished, and
" as my companion did not like the idea of going on short
" rations for a day or two, on the chance of getting goat, to
" my great regret we had to start for Horse-Thief Creek.
" The trail was very bad most of the way, and for the last
" few miles led through second-growth spruce which had
" been burnt the last year, just enough to kill it and no
" more. Any one who has travelled through this would
" understand that with pack-ponies, it was not all pleasure.
" We rode across Horse-Thief Creek where the trail struck
" it, and camped on the other side, on a nice flat with
" plenty of goose-grass for the ponies, so we knew they
" would not stray, and only hobbled them. It was a lovely
" moonlight night, and we were all soon asleep. I woke
" about midnight, and heard something splashing in the
" creek, but thinking it was only some of the ponies
" drinking, or crossing the water to another bank of goose-
" grass we had come through from the other side, I slept
" until morning. On turning out, I went down to the
" creek to see if any ponies had crossed, and there found

"the tracks of a large grizzly, and which I could have easily
"shot in the bright moonlight, if I had known it was a bear.

"*October* 16*th*.—Started early for Windermere. We met
"Baptiste's son before we got to Toby Creek; he was
"starting with Susan Margeau, the girl who searched for
"berries, to come and find us and hunt the ground beyond
"where we were camped; but Baptiste told them to return.
"We reached the hotel at Windermere about two o'clock,
"and to my great delight my wife arrived shortly after.

"This trip proves the truth of my opinion that, unless
"one knows the country oneself, and is not tied to time,
"it is little good hunting here. I am certain that,
"knowing the country as I do now, I could have good
"sport even alone, if I return, and choose my own time
"and place. I have lost six weeks of the best season for
"hunting, owing to a friend not having been able to get
"hunters engaged for me as he had expected; this has
"entirely spoiled my sport.

"*October* 17*th*.—We stopped to-day in the steamer at
"a wooding-stage, and to my surprise, were hailed from
"the bank by Moulson, a miner and hunter whom I knew.
"On hearing I had had no sport, he was very anxious I
"should come ashore, and go on a hunt with him, and that
"my wife should also come. I thought it too rough a trip
"for her; so with my blankets and a change in my kit-
"bag and my stalking-glass over my shoulder, I said
"good-bye to her, and jumped ashore with my rifle,
"leaving her to go down to Banff to await me there.

"Moulson had two horses and all his cooking-kit, so I
"left mine on the boat. We hoped to hit off my ponies
"on the trail, but the rascal we got to ride them down
"did the whole seventy miles in the half-day and night,
"so had passed, as we found on getting to the trail and
"inspecting the tracks. We sleep to-night at Macmillan's
"'shack,' a few miles from where I came ashore.

"*October* 18*th*.—We packed one horse and I rode the
"other, while Moulson walked. We reached Whisky Hill
"about mid-day, and camped on the river, which ran close
"below it. After picketing the horse we took a look round,
"but saw no tracks. Moulson's reason for coming here was
"that he knew it to be a great spring hunting-place for
"sheep, and he hoped, as no Indians were now hunting
"here, that we should get sheep high up in the range. I
"find him an excellent hunter and first-rate climber.
"The ground here is much more difficult and dangerous
"than where I have just come from, on Horse-Thief Creek.
"We are now in the Rockies, and the high ground we
"are hunting over is full of precipices and cañons, re-
"quiring care and good nerves to enable one to get about.
"I have done no big climbing for many years, and was
"afraid I should not be any good, but after the first few
"hours, found I could get along as well as in the old days.

"*October* 19*th*.—We started early, breakfasting before
"daylight, and hunted all over Whisky Hill, a huge
"mountain of granite, broken up by cañons in all directions,

"and split in two longitudinally, by one of great depth.
" The latter was a surprise to us, and when we had cruised
" over all the ground on this side of it, we had to descend
" and start up the other half of the mountain, so to speak,
" which meant a good deal of extra climbing. When we
" reached the top, or rather a flat just on the edge of the
" timber, as the real top was a bare peak of granite, it
" looked just the ground for sheep, as there was plenty of
" grass, water, and lots of sheltered ledges, which they like
" to lie in, but not a sheep nor a track did we see.

" The scenery was beautiful—range after range of snowy
" peaks in every direction, and the Columbia, from the
" upper lake down to Golden, winding along the valley.

" Below us flocks of geese and ducks were flying up and
" down, but we noticed that the geese were leaving for the
" south, which was a sure sign winter would be on us in a
" few days.

" Moulson is disgusted at having brought me to a place
" with no game in it; so we have decided to move down to
" Washout Creek to-morrow, as there we shall be nearer
" to the main range.

" *October 20th.*—Moved camp and turned the horses
" loose, having belled one of them, for we knew they would
" work down to their old range near Macmillan's shack.
" We fixed up camp near a nice creek, about half a mile
" back from the trail, and then took a short turn to see our
" best route for to-morrow; it looks bad, as the creek we
" are camped on is cañoned a mile from the mouth, and the

" mountains on either side are split lengthways by cañons
" with wall sides every mile or so, each of which we shall
" have to go round, after hunting the ground between them.

" *October 21st.*—Started at daylight; climbed up to the
" left of the creek. Spent the whole day hunting over
" almost impracticable ground, and found not a single track.
" Got to camp late, and started in the dark for Macmillan's.
" Caught the horses and got some food, and returned with
" both; the horses we had to picket for fear of their going
" back, but we have brought some oat-straw for them, so
" they held out pretty well.

" *October 22nd.*—It snowed, froze, and rained alternately
" most of the night. Packed one horse, and we went 'ride
" and tie' on the other. The weather did not improve,
" but was if possible worse. We made twenty-two miles,
" and camped close to the Hay ranche. The worst camp
" we have had, but we got beef and potatoes, so we lived
" well. If there only comes a really heavy storm, we
" ought to get sheep now, if there are any on the range.
" Two tepós of Shushwaps here, and the usual lot of
" papooses and cur-dogs; the latter are fearful thieves.
" The Indians have been hunting further down the river,
" and are now taking a band of ponies packed with their
" winter supply of flour up to where they live. We went
" and had a talk with them, and I took the opportunity to
" get a squaw to do some mending for me, as they sew
" buckskin beautifully with sinew, which is the only thing

" which stands hard work, and I had none, as we have
" killed no game.

" *October* 23rd.—Heavy rain and snow all night; looked
" like lasting all day too. It cleared about 3 P.M.—a good
" sign for our chances to-morrow. We dined sumptuously
" on beef and boiled beans, but, for some unknown reason,
" the latter made us both feel wretchedly ill.

" *October* 24th.—We turned out at 2.30 A.M., got breakfast,
" and walked to the foot of the range over some awfully
" swampy ground covered with alders—never very good
" going, but in the dark and covered with fresh snow, it was
" no holiday. We there lit a fire and waited for daylight,
" which appeared in about an hour. We had noticed one
" deer trail fresh in the snow, and that was all. We now
" started up the mountain—a very hard climb at any time,
" but, with six inches of fresh snow, it was really queer
" work, and we both were feeling very ill. On reaching the
" top we found our climb useless, as we were separated from
" the good ground by a wall cañon several hundred feet
" deep, so we had to retrace our steps, and were too seedy
" to do anything but return to camp.

" A miner staying at the ranch had found a keg of
" whisky *cachéd* in the potato-ground. He must have had
" a wonderful nose for spirit to find it in such an unlikely
" place; having found it, he had some out, and we annexed
" a portion, and had it hot and strong and full of pepper,
" which did us both good.

"On the way back I shot three grouse, which we stewed, and they made us an excellent supper.

"*October 26th.*—I was very ill all night, but slept in the
"morning. Another heavy snowstorm; stopped in camp
"and wrote a letter for the discoverer of the whisky.
"In the evening we packed a blanket a-piece, a kettle, an
"axe, tea and bread, and started up the mountain. I shot
"a grouse on the way, and we camped high up. A cold
"night, but we found dry cedar to burn, so we had a warm
"camp under a rock.

"Started over the mountain at daybreak; there was now
"a lot of snow, and we had a rough climb, but saw no
"tracks, though it looked excellent ground for game. We
"worked back to our fire by 2 P.M., packed our blankets,
"and started for camp, having made up our minds that
"there were no sheep here at this time of year. I shot a
"grouse on the way down, and with beef, potatoes, stewed
"fruit, and rice, we made up for our disappointment as
"regards sport, by an excellent dinner.

"*October 27th.*—We packed the horse, and took the
"trail as far as a shack five miles from Golden, where we
"stopped for the night, as the horses were about played
"out, for the snow had balled all day, and the trail was
"terrible going. I shot two grouse, which were useful for
"supper.

"*October 28th.*—It had snowed all night, and was at it

"as hard as ever this morning, but soon after daylight we packed our horse, and made for Golden, arriving about eleven o'clock.

"Here I settled accounts with Moulson, with whom I was quite sorry to part; he was a charming companion, and first-rate in the mountains. He takes care of Chance and Baldie, our two ponies, till next year, when I hope to return, and at 5.30 I take the cars for Banff, arriving at 11.30."

October 28th, Banff Springs Hotel, Rocky Mountains.—(I now resume my own journal where I left off at page 218). Met pleasant people here, who told us much that interested us about their travels in Cashmere, Mongolia, and other out-of-the-way places.

While we were all talking in the drawing-room after dinner, the editor of some Chicago newspaper introduced himself, bowing first to me. "Mrs. St. Maur, I believe?" I told him I was Mrs. St. Maur. He then said, "I have come to ask whether you were perfectly satisfied with the article I wrote about your fishing in the Minnewanka Lake. Was the description of the gaffing of the 28-lb. trout correct?"

Only two days previously I had been shown the article referred to for the first time. So far as I could judge, it was chiefly a family history of Algernon and myself, the 28-lb. trout only occupying a secondary place in the narrative. How he had found out anything about us puzzled me. It was badly written, and when, on our return to England, I heard it, or part of it, had been copied into the *Field*, we were exceedingly annoyed.

Here was a dilemma. But had I not appeared satisfied, something more distasteful might have been written. So I answered briefly, and thanked him. Fortunately he had to catch a train—his train for Chicago,—and that was the last we saw of him.

It was not the last we heard of him, for the C——s recognised him as having been one of their fellow-travellers on their journey from Vancouver. At one of the places where they stopped to dine, this Yankee got out with them for dinner. The "menu," which was written in French, was not legible. Mrs. C—— remarked to her husband that she could not read it. The editor immediately joined in their conversation from the other side of the table, saying, " I guess, in the States we do all our chewing in English ; I like to know what my victuals are when I eat them." When one considers that the article on our fishing had been written by this untutored person, was it to be wondered at that it did not quite suit my fancy ?

October 29*th*.—A busy day, putting all our wardrobes into order. When there is an accumulation of mending to be done, it is then one misses a maid. Fortunately for me, there were two nice Scotch girls in the hotel, who were concerned with the temporary management. One of them, I believe for the sole reason that I was from the "auld countree," took away a great pile of Algernon's stockings, and brought them back beautifully mended.

October 30*th*.—We walked through the woods, very rough going, as the only trail is where the trees have been cut about one foot from the ground; these stumps catch one's petticoat (though it be very short), impeding progress; and there was deep snow as well.

October 31*st*.—A glorious day; tried another sketch of these wonderful mountains with indifferent success. In the afternoon drove with two people staying here to the "Minnewanka Lake." Saw a cayote on the way there, but he was too quick for Algernon, and before he was out of the waggonette with his rifle, had disappeared into the woods.

At the lake, the boatman thought there was an off-chance of a wild sheep, so Algernon remained there for the night in order to hunt at early dawn. We had a funny little tea-party in a warm log-house, before we started for our return journey. A gentleman's house! for we saw at once our host was such, though he was at some pains to conceal his identity. Ah! how fond mothers at home would grieve, were they to see some of their dear sons out here, getting along as best they can! There is this difference, however; here no one is ashamed of working, and the free life makes men content.

"Here Life the undiminished man demands,
New faculties stretch out to meet new wants,
What nature asks, that nature also grants,
Here man is lord, not drudge, of eyes and feet and hands,
And to his life is knit with hourly bands."

A wooden hotel is being built here, and will be available for sportsmen next spring; the only tenant at present is a mountain rat, who lives in the unlighted stove. Now a rat I have a great antipathy to at any time, but when two cats were taken into the empty room, where he was to be exhibited, I was inspired with confidence. Seeing a high wooden table in the corner of the room, Mrs. B—— and I chose this as our point of observation, sitting after the fashion of Turkish ladies. The mountain rat was let out of his temporary home—the stove; a creature much larger than an English rat, with a bushy tail, came out and ran so fast, that a doubt was expressed as to where he had gone. From our vantage-ground, the table, we heard an unpleasant suggestion that the rat was behind us. In an instant we were both out of the room, and preferred a view of this interesting animal through the window. The two cats did not attack, they only ran after it!

Our drive back to the hotel through the mountains was beautiful; all descriptions would fail to tell of what we saw: far below us in the valley the little mountain stream, half frozen in the arms of its strange nurse winter, shining all along the silvery way it had mapped out for itself. Among the grey rocks, half covered with snow, were many frozen waterfalls, seemingly arrested in their course, and transfixed into thousands of icicles, while towering mountain ranges with snowy peaks seemed to surround us on all sides.

CHAPTER XVIII.

THE PRAIRIE—WINNIPEG—MOOSE-HUNTING—MANITOBA.

"The wild free woods make no man halt or blind,
Cities rob men of eyes and hands and feet."—*Lowell.*

Banff Springs Hotel, Rocky Mountains, November 2nd.—
The guardian of the National Park told me the following
anecdote of the Stony Indians. When he first arrived
here everything was in a state of disorder, not a house in
the place, and his party were in tents and not too well
stocked with provisions. Under these circumstances it
was deemed advisable not to encourage the Indians, who
from time to time came round begging for food, but to
refuse to give them anything. However, late one afternoon an Indian arrived with his squaw and papoose and a
little boy; they had evidently come a long way, and
when food was refused the small child began to cry,
and the Indian gave him his pipe, which is supposed to
allay the pangs of hunger. On seeing that they were
really in need, Mr. Stewart ordered them a dish of food;
before touching it they sat down, and, closing their eyes,
asked their grace. The sight of starving people not

forgetful to thank their Father above for His mercies could not fail to impress any one who witnessed the scene. What bright and simple faith was theirs! Is it not true

> "That in even savage bosoms
> There are longings, yearning, strivings,
> For the good they comprehend not,
> That the feeble hands, and helpless,
> Groping blindly in the darkness
> Touch God's right hand in that darkness?"

I was told of a Blackfoot Indian who the other day got into the cars at one of the prairie stations. After a time he signed to some man to ask if he could get anything to eat; the man thus questioned gave him a dinner in the dining-car. The Indian was much pleased, and maintained a most dignified demeanour throughout, but looked round to see how he should use his knife and fork, which he then managed just as well as the other people who were dining round him. An Indian considers it undignified ever to seem surprised, and is seldom in a hurry.

When the railway was being built, the things which pleased the Indians most were the Clydesdale horses, as they had never seen anything larger than their own bronchos; but here were horses seventeen hands high! They sat looking at them with the greatest astonishment, and a Kootenay, who was mounted on one, returned to his tribe with such wonderful stories of the size and breadth of the great English horses that they laughed at him, thinking he spoke nonsense.

Royal Hotel, Winnipeg, November 8th.—We left Banff

some days ago for Mitford, where we arrived at 3 in the morning. It was not very pleasant turning out of the warm cars at that hour, and finding oneself on the snow-covered prairie, with a cutting wind and hard frost. Fortunately E. W—— knew we were coming, and we found him waiting for us with a lantern, our only light until we got to the new hotel, which has been built and furnished since we were here last. We were glad to get to bed, though I was so thoroughly chilled that I could not get warm all the rest of the night.

Next morning after breakfast we took a twelve-mile walk, first to the coal-mine, and afterwards to Cochrane and back, leaving for Calgary at the same dismal hour, 3 A.M., at which we had arrived. We spent half the night and the next day there, as Algernon had some business to attend to, and then left at 3.18 A.M.

Three very cold and broken nights had quite tired me out, and I found two days in the cars to Winnipeg comparatively restful.

The prairie in June and the prairie in November are woefully unlike. In June all was green and bright; the glorious summer, with all its hope and joy, had plenty in store for our pleasure. Now it looked bare, and gloomy, and hopeless; the prairie towns seemed like belated travellers, camping until they found better things, the thin frame houses in straight stiff rows appearing ill fitted to keep out the piercing cold.

Of game on the prairie one sees little or none from the cars; the shrill whistle of the locomotive over the wide expanse and in the once silent mountain valleys has sounded the death-knell of the splendid big game of North America.

We reached Winnipeg at 6 P.M., and were not sorry to find ourselves there and to have a good rest.

November 9th.—We went to see the opening of the House of Legislature for the province of Manitoba this afternoon, and were pointed out some of the principal men. We heard the leader of the Government, Mr. Greenaway, make his opening speech—a defence of himself and other members of the Government, who had been accused of bribery in one of the Winnipeg papers.

The most remarkable person we saw was Mons. Narquet, a half-breed, a most able man, who for fifteen years had been premier, but this year, on his Government going out, was leader of the Opposition.* He was by far the most eloquent member of the House, and very proud of his Indian descent. In a former session he was jeered at for this by a Scotchman, who should have known better. Narquet's reply, however, was so dignified that it silenced any further remarks, and left the member who had attacked him somewhat humiliated; it was to this effect, "that he was proud of the Scotch blood in his veins, but still prouder of his Indian descent, knowing that an attack of the description to which he had been subjected would never have been made by an Indian."

There is a most excellent library and museum attached

* Mons. Narquet died this year.

to the House of Legislature, and any one in the Province of Manitoba having an order from a member can make use of them.

While in Winnipeg we were shown a charming private collection of Indian curios—beautiful bead-work, some of the patterns looking quite Oriental. The broad ribbons of bead-work have the patterns the same on both sides, the combination of colours being harmonious and well chosen. The work done by the half-breeds is inferior in every way, the work being coarser and the colours harsher in tone. From whence have these isolated Indian tribes got their Oriental patterns?

We paid an interesting visit to the Hudson's Bay Company's stores, which stand almost on the site of the Old Fort Garry, of which only the old gateway now remains. The stores are able to supply everything one can think of. All kinds of provisions, furs, ironmongery, and machinery, can be bought there, and all of good quality. Winnipeg is the great commercial centre of this western country. As I passed the millinery department with Paris fashions in hats and bonnets, I thought how different must Old Fort Garry have been, when the trade consisted principally in outfitting the company's hunters, and receiving in the spring the proceeds of their hunt, or in trading goods to strange Indians and hunters in barter for furs, and other native produce.

Our train left at 6 P.M., and we had to hurry our preparations, and obtain another supply of camp-kit, in the way of kettles, and provisions, as Algernon had set his heart on getting a moose if possible before we went home. We have heard of a place where there is a good chance, if it will only snow a little.

Algernon went to the Hudson's Bay Stores, and as he knew exactly what he wanted and they are used to outfitting hunters every day, he soon had all he required packed in a case, and sent to the "depôt," as the station is called.

On our way to the station, we stopped at the taxidermist's shop; he is setting up a head for me. I never saw such a fine collection of heads. He had two splendid buffalo, the last they are ever likely to get. One, shot near Swift Current a few months ago, was for sale for $100. The price asked did not seem excessive when one considers the value of an auk's egg! He also had very fine specimens of moose, elk, caribou, wild sheep, timber wolves, goat, mule, deer, and lynx. We also saw in the town many specimens of this season's furs.

Arrived at the station, with vague ideas of our destination, in bitterly cold weather, so that I was very glad of a large rabbit robe which had kindly been lent to me.

Algernon has not even seen his hunter yet, but he was taken by a man to a bootmaker's shop; the bootmaker said his friend, who was in the shop, was friend of the man who would take us hunting! This sounded rather complicated. The bootmaker and his friend, who showed most kind interest in our preparations, both arrived at the station "on time," as they say here, and after our "kit" was all checked to one place, on second thoughts they changed our destination. By "kit" I mean blankets, provisions, tent, rifles, kettles, and the everlasting frying-pan; all our other baggage we had checked through to Ottawa, to await our arrival there.

It is very pleasant to see how people out here, who know little or nothing about us, put themselves to the greatest trouble and inconvenience to help us if they can.

We found ourselves before morning on the platform of a little wayside station, *en route* for the happy hunting-grounds. My heart certainly failed me at Winnipeg—it seemed almost a wildgoose chase, but my failing spirits revived here, when we found ourselves at a charming little clean wooden hotel, and heard one man after another say that there was a good chance for moose.

Here, as at Winnipeg, the men all tried to dissuade me from going with Algernon, saying it was too rough; but having experienced the horrors of being left behind so often, I determined at all risks to keep with him.

So many men we have seen this year have had little or no sport; this is very disappointing, but if one were always successful, there would not be the same excitement.

Hunting moose requires the greatest skill; they possess the keenest powers of smell and hearing, and if they get the slightest scent of the hunter, or if he snaps even a twig within their hearing, they are off, and sometimes do not stop for twelve hours or more. Algernon, who has hunted them a great deal in New Brunswick, says it is a curious fact that they seem to distinguish at once between the snapping of a bough caused by a storm in the woods, and that caused by persons striking one or treading on it. Their food consists of willows, dogwood, and, if they cannot get these, young birch; the dogwood they prefer. They also browse on the young wood of other hardwood trees, but the two mentioned are their staple food; they therefore live principally in swampy ground, and in summer prefer the neighbourhood of a lake or river, in which they will often stand for hours with nothing out of the water but their heads, so as to avoid the bites of the mosquitoes and moose-fly.

There are three ways of hunting moose: calling, still-hunting or creeping, and running them down on snow-shoes.

Calling begins the first full moon in September; few white men and for that matter few Indians are good callers. The call is given through a birch-bark horn; the hunter selects, if possible, a small lake with open meadow round it, or a wide grassy creek side, in the neighbourhood of which he knows there are moose; he gets to this place just before sundown, and after selecting a position so that as much of the open ground as possible shall be out of shadow of the surrounding trees when the moon rises, and also commanded by the rifle, which is generally in the hands of a companion, waits till the sun is down, and then usually climbs a convenient tree, so that the sound may carry further. He now gives the call, a most wild complaining kind of cry, which can be heard two or three miles in the still evening; perhaps he may get no answer, but if there are moose in the neighbourhood, as a rule an answer will be heard in half an hour or so, if the call has been given correctly. Sometimes after the answer another call has to be given, but generally this does more harm than good. The caller now descends, and if alone prepares for a shot, if with a friend, joins him and keeps watch. The most perfect silence must be maintained, and on no account must the hunter move, as a twig cracking when the moose comes is enough to cause him to glide silently away, which he will do in the thickest underwood without making a sound. Often one hears the moose coming for a mile, smashing the dead branches, and breaking down everything in his way, making a novice think that twenty moose are coming instead of one. When, however, he arrives within about 200 yards, he generally stops and becomes suspicious, and, if possible, tries to get to leeward of the spot from which the call proceeded; if he succeeds in this, he is of course gone directly; if not, the caller gives a low call which is most difficult, as half a note out is enough to undeceive the moose: but if all goes well, the bull will now walk and often trot right out into the open, straight to where the hunter is concealed, when, if the light is not too bad, a bullet drops him dead at fifty yards.

Still-hunting, or creeping, is really the most sportsmanlike way of killing moose, and likewise the most difficult, and consists of stalking him in his feeding-ground, which is generally of a swampy nature, thickly covered with willows

MORE ABOUT MOOSE.

and other growth. It is almost hopeless to attempt this, except in moccasins, and then a " tenderfoot," which is what they call one new to the country out here, will generally find he has given the moose his wind, as moose almost invariably before settling to feed or rest, which they generally do standing up, take care to get to leeward of their own trail, so that a hunter not up to this always gives them his wind; whilst any one used to the sport keeps working well to leeward of the trail, and so catches the moose unawares. If once alarmed moose will, generally travel from twelve to twenty-four hours without a halt, and at their usual trot soon put thirty or forty miles between themselves and their enemies.

Chasing on snow-shoes when the snow is over $2\frac{1}{2}$ or 3 feet deep is of course no sport, but simply murder, and should be stopped by law, but with $1\frac{1}{2}$ feet of good snow the hunter and the moose are about equally matched; it is then a question of great patience, endurance, and perseverance to kill a moose in this way.

Algernon says, " We used if possible to find out where a " moose-yard was, and try and start the moose just at " daybreak; if there were three or four, we would pick the " biggest by the tracks, and start after him at a steady trot. " The moose always chooses the roughest ground; it makes " no difference to him, and bothers the hunter a good deal. " If the hunter is in good condition, the moose can " generally be run to a stand-still by sundown.

" It is best on getting up to the moose to sit down and " get one's wind before attempting to shoot him, as after a

" hard day like this one otherwise makes a very bad shot.
" A good feed of moose liver broiled on the fire while you
" skin him soon puts you right for the tramp home to camp
" by moonlight, with some of the meat packed on your back
" or in the hide, which is used as a temporary toboggan;
" the rest you probably fetch next day."

CHAPTER XIX.

LIFE IN A LUMBER-CAMP.

"The roaring camp fire with rude humour painted
The ruddy tints of health."—*Lowell*.

The Woods, Manitoba, November.—A sledge drawn by two horses arrived, and on it were soon firmly fastened our provisions, blankets, and other things.

The trail was very bad, and part of the way lay through burnt woods, but some of the swamps we had to pass over were fortunately frozen hard. One of the men going on with us told us that the day before, when coming out of the woods, he had seen a fine moose, but had not his rifle with him.

A few miles from the camp we had to cross a river in a tub of a boat, and after making the best of our way through more "muskegs" and over rough ground, just as it was getting dark we came in sight of the lumber-camp. As none of my sex—except the doctor, who happens to be a woman—had ever been up to a lumber-camp in this part of the country, my arrival caused much surprise. One of the men who were standing about the door of the camp when we appeared ran in, saying, "By ——, here's "a woman!"

I must confess when I reached the inside I wished myself back at Winnipeg. A large fire of piled logs burnt on a raised hearth in the centre of the camp, the smoke escaping by a hole in the roof. When we entered the only light was from this huge fire, which threw a ruddy glow on the rows of weather-beaten faces which surrounded it. The men seemed of many nationalities— Germans, Norwegians, Finlanders, Americans, Canadians, and Scotchmen, and their fine physique testified to the health of the life they were leading.

Great disappointment was expressed that no one had brought a newspaper. The Americans were interested in the elections now going on in the States, and even here party-feeling seemed to run high. It is difficult to describe the pleasure which books and papers give to these men, as there are always two or three hours in which they have nothing to do before bed-time. For this reason the few books in a camp are read and re-read many times.

One of the men told me that he had worked for a time on Lord Lansdowne's ranch, and there the men were given a good supply of books. He said once he had as many as eighty of his own, but they got lost, "some of the boys" borrowing them and forgetting to return them.

The camp itself is a low log building, oblong in shape, with rough bunks in two tiers running round three sides of it; and on the fourth side is the large cooking-stove and the cook's shelves and table, holding plates, dishes, cooking utensils, and food. Suspended on poles run over the cross-beams in the roof were the men's wet gloves, and socks, drying, and each man kept in his bunk or under it, his box or bag, containing his extra clothes and his few other possessions. There are two doors, one at the back, and the other in front of the house.

After resting awhile, we heard the sledge with our "kit" arriving, and went out to get our things off. Then Algernon and the foreman of the camp, who was going to hunt with him, pitched our tent about 200 yards from the lumber camp, on the top of a little hill, some of the other men good-naturedly giving assistance, and cutting up a supply of firewood for us. The foreman lent us an old tent, which we put over our own, thus doubling the thickness of the canvas; he also lent us a sheet-iron stove, which we put at the end of the tent nearest to the door, and which, when lighted, made the inside very warm in a few minutes. An even temperature in a tent is impossible to maintain; it is either very hot or very cold. Some rough hay from the stables was put under our blankets, and as we had plenty of the latter and rabbit-robes, we felt we should sleep well. The stove soon burnt brightly; we had our kettle boiling and supper cooking in half an hour. We hung up our lamp by a string from the ridge pole, so had a pleasant light in our little tent; then I was glad to stretch myself out, weary as I then was, on the blankets and rugs, which made a capital sofa *pro tem.*, for we had had a long day, and we were both tired.

November 13th.—At 5.30 in the morning Algernon started with his hunter after moose: to him, therefore, fell the task of preparing breakfast.

After they were gone I put on a long pair of dogskin gloves, and then began my duties. The first thing was to arrange the inside of the tent, to fold up the blankets, and place everything in its own place; if this be not done, then all the comfort of tent-life is at an end, because nothing can be found when wanted.

Luncheon I was supposed to get for myself, but bread and marmalade are enough, and I drink water rather than have the trouble of boiling the kettle. With a hungry hunter to be fed at night it is a very different matter, and I always prepare a very good supper before Algernon's return. The cook at the camp with whom I have made friends, makes excellent bread and cakes for us daily, thus saving me all the trouble of baking; and any of the other men who are about the camp are most anxious to do anything to help me, and they seem very much pleased if I talk to them about their homes and people.

I took one of the men with me, and went off to shoot some rabbits with my rifle. I got four. One of these I exchanged at the lumber-camp for a partridge, and the cook was good enough to prepare the other three for the pot. I then set to work, and this was our *menu* at supper.

> Rabbit Broth.
> Grilled Partridge.
> Baked Potatoes.
> Stewed Apricots.
> Rice Pudding.

(We drank nothing but tea while in camp.)

The hunters returned—no moose! The weather they say is too fine; there has been just a sprinkling of snow but not enough to prevent them from making too much noise in travelling through the woods. To-day they came on the fresh tracks of a moose that they had disturbed.

Just as we were beginning supper, a hand was thrust into the tent door with a large plate full of buns—a most welcome addition.

I saw the first snow-birds to-day; the moose-birds, of which there seem many round the camp, are wonderfully tame; the latter seem rather like jackdaws in their ways, the same sort of independent birds; indeed when the weather is cold and food scarce they will eat out of one's hand. They are called by the men Whisky-Jacks, and bear a charmed life for the most part, as they are thought lucky about a camp; they are pretty birds about the size of a jay and of a bluish-grey colour.

The rabbits here do not burrow, but hide under the brush and in hollow logs; they resemble the blue hare, and like him turn snow-white in winter. Poor little fellows! so much of the brush was burnt by last year's fire that they find it rather hard to hide themselves until there is a fall of snow. The Sauteaux Indians make their skins into beautiful robes, which are so warm that when rolled in one of them no cold can penetrate. It takes about 500 skins to make a good robe. The skins are plaited into ropes with the hair outwards on both

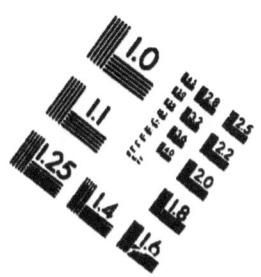

**IMAGE EVALUATION
TEST TARGET (MT-3)**

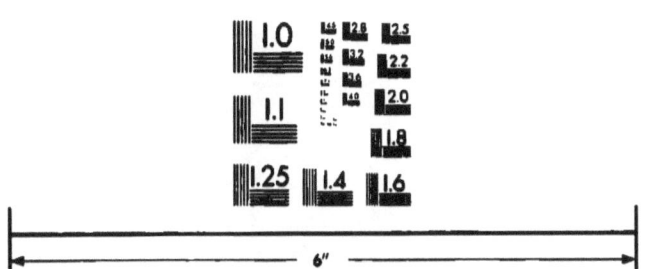

Photographic
Sciences
Corporation

23 WEST MAIN STREET
WEBSTER, N.Y. 14580
(716) 872-4503

sides, and then these ropes are fastened together until the robe is the right size: one can put one's fingers through it anywhere.

The little squirrels and chipmunks scold me as I pass along under the bare trees and wander about for hours at a time with them as my only companions.

Last night I heard one little squirrel very busy making a raid on our provisions; I did not grudge him his share so long as he did not invite his uncles, his cousins, and his aunts to assist him, for I fear then the store-house would not have withstood the strain.

The man who owns all this lumbering business here is married to a daughter of Whitehead the engineer, who helped to drive the first locomotive in England with George Stephenson. Whitehead still lives, a hale old man of eighty-six years, and sometimes comes to pay his daughter a visit. He lives in the States, and from his association with Stephenson was looked upon as such a celebrity, and so many came to see him in consequence, that he had to build a high fence round his house to shut himself off from the too curious public.

This morning Algernon and his hunter wished to start very early because they knew exactly where the moose were; so Algernon woke me at 5.30 A.M.

One sleeps here with one's head well under the blankets and furs, because of the intense cold. My first thought, What a cold morning! and so it was. All water frozen solid in the tent, but with the aid of the stove, which we soon have blazing, we get up some degree of heat, and after breakfast felt quite warm.

A glorious morning, but snow is required for hunting, and of course the snow has not come.

There are moose-tracks all round, but it is impossible to get near them without making a noise, more especially as we are in the midst of burnt woods; for this reason Algernon and W—— returned at 12 o'clock, as they were anxious not to frighten these moose off the ground.

We arranged the tent, and I obtained a supply of water for our day's requirements at the creek. The stream is all frozen over, but by dipping one's can through a hole in the ice one can get some out, the danger being (from the slippery state of the ground) the probability of following the can into the hole. It is somewhat of a novel experience this winter camp-life to me. The squirrels, ermine, chipmunks, snowbirds, woodpeckers, and moosebirds all eye me curiously as an intruder into their dominions, and so I doubtless am. How tame they are! they hop round the camp-door or the tent-door; it amuses me to watch them. One little brown squirrel with a straight brush of a tail, not like the feathery tails of our English squirrels, is provisioning his camp for the winter with a cold potato, which seems rather a big load; he moves off with considerable difficulty, having fastened the potato into his two upper teeth, and by holding his head very far back he just manages it. Wise squirrel! in a few weeks the lumber-camp moves ten miles further into the bush, as by that time the men will have finished cutting the logs here, and the chances of a further harvest for him will have gone.

The men call the ermine white weasels; their little coats are familiar to me, I have seen them frequently on muffs and used as the lining of cloaks. These tiny creatures will often go into the camps and eat out of the men's hands, even take crumbs out of their pockets, and these lonely lumbermen seem to love animals and will seldom do them any harm.

I am greatly struck with the happy contentment of the men; the majority appear to wish for nothing more than their circumstances allow, and rarely do they change their employment.

It is quite a pleasure to see an expert lumberman wield his axe; he does make the chips fly, and the axe seems never to rest, but to be swung round with the most perfect ease as each blow falls. Not until a new hand has been two winters in the woods is he considered to have had sufficient practice to use it properly.

Some raw rabbit meat froze solid, so that we had to cut it off the tin dish with an axe. People do not know the power of frost at home; I only record these trivial incidents as they have never occurred to me before.

The lumbermen have come out in their winter clothing. They mostly wear *capotes*, a red cap the same as the *bonnet rouge* at the time of the French Revolution, doubtless brought into the country by the early French settlers, and made of blue or red wool; they pull these over the ears if necessary. They also wear over their ordinary clothing long red duffel stockings, and over them, boots lined with flannel. Their hands have to be kept constantly covered with great warm buckskin mits; these have one place for all the fingers and thumb, like a baby's glove. All this extra clothing costs a great deal—these mits $2 (over 8s.) a pair, and with the hard work they do not last long. One of the men tells me his boots and overboots cost him $100 a year.

At the lumber-camp the foreman keeps two large chests filled with blankets, mits, caps, trousers, jerseys, tobacco, all the goods the men are likely to want; he even has watches. All this encourages thrift among them. He sometimes sells as much as $4,000 worth during a winter. Many of the men arrive totally unprovided with the necessary clothes for this out-of-door life; these are speedily supplied from the chests, and the price deducted from their wages.

If snow would only come, then moose would easily be obtained, as they are in the woods all round this camp, but with hard frost and little or no snow, every sound, even the breaking of the tiniest twig in this keen air, makes a noise like a pistol-shot. We wake each morning, expecting to find the ground thickly covered with snow, in which case the hunters would have a good chance; they are out all and every day as it is, but have not yet had one shot.

After we have finished supper in the evenings, we often hear a voice outside—Algernon's hunter—asking how we are getting along, if we are cold, if we have enough of everything. Algernon invites him to come in and have a talk. He is foreman of the lumber-camp, and an excellent hunter as well. I ask for bear stories.

"Yes! oh yes! there are," he says, "lots of bears round here, but all are hybernating now."

"Do you never come across them during the winter?"

"One time we were clearing a new trail for hauling logs, and under a great tree stump which they were removing the boys came upon no less than four together. The men seemed startled for a moment; I ran off to fetch my gun, and shot two of them; one escaped into the woods, and one took up a tree, and a half-breed tomahawked him. An old hunter who is here had his foot clawed by a wounded bear. He had to run, and took refuge in a tree, which was too small, and his leg hung down too near the bear: finally her attention was diverted by a dog, and she left him; for which, as he had dropped his rifle, he was not sorry."

These men's lives are full of hardships and adventure, consequently they do not seem to think much of a fuss with a bear.

When Algernon was in Colorado some years ago, he went to a log-house one day, where he found the owner in bed. He knew the man, and asked what was the matter. It appeared that he had set a trap in the alder-brush near his house for a bear which had been about there for some days. Going to look at it the morning before Algernon paid this visit, he found a cub in the trap. He went to knock it on the head, but it began to cry. The old bear was up in the brush close by, and charged directly. The man fired at her with one of the old small-bore Kentucky rifles, and as it turned out afterwards, shot her through the heart; but she did not mind, and came on. He ran for his life, but tripped over an alder root. She caught him at once, biting him through one shoulder and both thighs, in which she made her teeth meet, and with a hind-foot took a strip of flesh off from his neck to the small of his back. His son, who had luckily gone with him, then killed the bear with a blow at the back of the head with the heavy barrel of the rifle. The man recovered, but a year after Algernon went to ask him to come bear-hunting with him. He replied that " he guessed he had " not lost any bears !"

Stream-driving, as floating the logs down the river to the mill or other destination is called, is the roughest work the lumbermen have. The foreman told me that from the time the drive starts until it arrives neither he nor any of the men have dry clothes on them day or night, and that for seventy-five days on last year's drive he never had more than four hours' sleep.

The foreman of a drive is always supposed to go at the head of it, which is the post of danger. As W—— said, "How can I put other men's lives in danger and not risk "my own?" He then told us the following story:—

"Well, two men came from New Brunswick who had " the reputation of being the best men on a drive in their " district. 27,000 logs had jammed on our river, and I " started in a canoe with them to break it. I told them I

s

"would break it with my axe, and they promised to pick me up; at the second blow of the axe off went the logs. I got back into the canoe, but the men scared, and jumped out on to a rock in the rapids. I was unable to manage the canoe alone, so canoe and I went over the falls with the logs, and she turned over. I was used to walking on logs—you see our driving boots have 112 spikes in them, which stick firm into a log when you jump on it—so I was able to jump from log to log until I reached the shore. The two men thought they had seen the last of me, but they hadn't, and I was able to tell them afterwards they weren't the right sort, and to dismiss them. When the boss heard of it, he said he would not have me run no such risks again, anyway not on his jams."

Two men cutting with a cross-saw and two men skidding with a team will, if timber grows fairly thick, cut and pile eighty logs in a day, while four men unaccustomed to the work will only manage half that number.

A few of the men here have farms in Ontario, which they have sublet, as they prefer working in the woods.

This is a wonderful country for the industrious working man. For $10 he can become the possessor of 160 acres of land, on condition that he builds a house, cultivates a certain amount of ground annually, and lives on it for six months in the year. He can select any unoccupied land, and for any extra quantity he may require he pays $2 per acre. A good log-house can be built for $150. Why then do not more of our surplus population emigrate to this country? Many of them could find the small sum necessary to bring them here and buy land; there is room for any number. But no, many who might come remain at home idle, coveting what is not theirs, too lazy to work, listening with willing ears to the gospel of spoliation preached by those who make a living by it, and who really do not care what becomes of their country or of their dupes.

It is cold at nights in spite of blankets and furs, as we have now $10°$ or $15°$ below zero. The heat of our bodies condenses on the outside of the rabbit robes, so that they are covered with a coating of ice in the morning.

Algernon's hunter is a fine example of how a workingman can get along if he will. He has taught himself to read and write, and amuses me when he talks of his wife. He seems to consider weight and size everything; telling me with evident pride she weighs over 200 lbs. He married her when she was fifteen and he two years older; he saw her first helping her father to clear a road to his homestead, which sounds rather hard work for a young woman. They have got on "just splendid," he says. Now he earns at the rate of $100 a month, and has the summer to himself. He owns over 400 acres near here, as well as his farm in Ontario. He evidently does not think with the old Scotch saying, "Good gear is put up in small bundles."

"Buccaro Jimmy" came up from the camp this morning with a book, thinking I might like "a bit of reading," Jimmy's idea of a delightful book being "Quick "and Dead," by Amelia Reeves. Its principal merit seemed to be that it was improbable and highly sensational.

I asked if he ever went to see his relations, and where they lived.

"Well," said Buccaro Jimmy, "I have not seen my people for nearly nine years, and they think me dead; anyway, it was in the newspapers I'd been killed by Indians when scouting."

"Why don't you write, or go home and see them?" I asked.

"I did go to the office where the old man was working after I'd been away three years. My own father looked up from his writing, and asked me what I wanted; he did not know me, so I just left, and have never been there again. I love the life on the plains, and as soon as the grass gets green again I shall go back there, but I prefer the States to Canada—it's more home-like."

Seemingly encouraged by my listening to him, he went on in a little while, as if he were thinking aloud. "What more does one want with all the woods around? But it's a hard life, I tell you, riding after the wild cattle on the plains, and loping along on a horse for days together, out in all weathers, and, as often as not, all night too. Yes, we like our rig" (meaning saddle, bridle, shaps, spurs, and lariat) "to be of the best. Mine are worth $360, and are lying at Winnipeg until I want them again. One time I lost a whole rig; my horse was drowned crossing the Snake River. It's very deep, you know, and a strong current, and while we were crossing he got carried off. I

"got hold of a cottonwood and pulled myself out, but I lost
"all that rig, and it was worth $300, and the horse too.
"When the spring comes, I'm going on one of Sir John
"Kaye's places. I guess there will be some bronchos to
"break there. Often when I've been breaking them in
"Montana, they've bucked till the blood came out of my
"nose, ears, and mouth, and it gives a man a pain here,"
putting his hand on his chest. "I like to travel. When
"I make $2,000 or $3,000 I go off for a trip; you see I
"don't care to drink or gamble, so I spend my money
"travelling. I've been to the Sandwich Islands and New
"Mexico, and think some day I'll go to South Africa to see
"that. Yes, we often get killed off, but that is because
"we are just out of luck."

Alas, poor Jimmy! I have since heard he both drank and gambled, and was a hardish case.

Such are the men daily met with here. I am told by W——, he has known a man to change his name six times in a year. No characters are necessary in a lumber camp; each stands on his own merits. No gambling is permitted, and the men have to go to bed at 9 o'clock. If they work well, they stay generally through the winter; if they are idle, they are paid off directly. They are comfortable and well fed, and can earn from $1½ to $2½ per day. The cost of boarding the men is about $2½ per week when well managed.

This evening one of the new hands, having given himself a holiday, came back with four bottles of whisky. After he had been put to bed, for the reason that he could not go himself, Karl, who is W——'s nephew, and who was in charge of the camp, poured out the contents of the bottles into the snow. In the morning the owner was frantic; but it is by these rough methods that good order is maintained.

Sunday, November 18*th.*—A calm, lovely and very frosty day. There is no work to do, so the men wander listlessly about. It really made me feel quite miserable that they had no one to speak to them of better things. At last I mustered up sufficient courage to offer to come and read to them. They accepted gladly, and at 7.30, after the supper was cleared away, I went to the camp, sat on a barrel near where the lamp hung, because half the camp seemed dark, and read the psalms and lessons for the day, and then talked to them about what I had read, and they were so quiet and attentive, one could not hear the slightest sound. We had several hymns, in which the men joined. I read each verse to them first, because they had not a Bible, prayer-book, nor hymn-book among them. The intense earnestness of some of their faces showed how much they felt even this little effort on their behalf.

When the big camp is started and there are 150 to 200 men at work, they have a weekly service.

Recklessness is their principal characteristic; they seem to think little and care less. In spite of this, however, there is much that is noble and to be admired in some of these lumbermen. They would share their last sixpence with any friend who required it, and they nurse each other when ill with the tenderness and gentle care of a woman.

November 19*th*.—Algernon was up very early. Just as I was dressing, the tent caught fire; it was caused by the ridge pole being too near the stove-pipe. Of course it all blazed up, and I had only just time to dash out, drawing my fur cloak over me as I went.

The men, fortunately for us, were just starting for work. The cry of "Fire" soon brought them running, and many willing hands extinguished the flames. Part of the tent was burned, but we were able to put it right with spare bits of canvas. We are glad that all our things were not destroyed.

When I came in this evening I found a corner of the tent again smouldering, but I put it out quite easily. Two fires in one day are rather alarming.

The foreman told me that last year a man arrived at the camp on a Sunday, and said that he had been sent by the Presbytery at Winnipeg. He asked him if he might hold a service for the men, to which he willingly consented. He then said it was customary after the service to make a collection, and that the Presbytery expected every man to give a dollar towards the expenses. To this the foreman said no, that the service might be held, but no money collected from the men. Afterwards the man tried to make him alter his decision, without success. He heard of him later going the round of other camps, collecting as much as $17 at one. To make a long story short, it was found that he was sent by no one at Winnipeg, but was a Yankee swindler from Montana, and that he had collected $400 in this way during the winter.

Karl, the young fellow who took me out shooting several times, I thought was a Norwegian, but he says he is an American. On asking him a little about his family, he told me that his mother came from Glasgow and his father from the Clyde, therefore I should have said he was Scotch. They, however, all like the privileges of American citizens.

Once, having gone to the lumber-camp to fetch something, I found the camp cook and foreman examining and sorting the letters for the morrow's post, and was amused at hearing the following dialogue. It must be remembered that from always being a very necessary person in camp, the cook not only holds an important post so far as the comfort of the men is concerned, but also, from being always at home, sees and knows all that goes on. On this occasion he seemed to take a great interest in the correspondence—not idle curiosity, but rather a fatherly interest in the well-doing of the camp.

"Whose letter is this?" asked the foreman, taking up a thick and closely written envelope.

"Oh," replied the cook, "that one is Jamie's letter to his sweetheart; it took him several evenings to write it all."

Many letters were looked over with passing remarks.

At last one seemed to puzzle them; it was firmly closed, with no address.

"That," said the cook, "must be Karl's letter, but he "does not wish us to know her name!"

They had not decided the probable destination of the letter when the door was burst open and Karl himself walked in, having shaken the snow from his rough clothing, which was, however, made picturesque by a red cap "toque," sash, and red duffel overall stockings. Standing before them 6 feet 4 without his boots, a picture of health and strength, with honesty and candour written on every line of his young face,—they asked him,—

"Whose letter is this?"

"It's mine!" replied Karl, "you can address it to my "mother!" *

The Canadian lumbermen so thoroughly understand their work, that in the States they are paid $10 a month more than any other men. Many out here squander their wages; happily there are exceptions. One young fellow who has been in the woods two years has saved over $300, bought a hundred and sixty acres of land, and owns a house besides, which he has sublet for $5 a month. He hopes in the spring to have out his father, mother, and sisters, "from the old country" to live with him. He told me he came from an estate in Forfarshire. This gives an idea of what any steady hardworking young man may do in this country, if he will.

* Poor Karl will have to get some one else to write his love-letters now, for alas! we hear that a gun accident has blown off his right hand!

November 21st.—Breakfast in our tent this morning at 5.30. No snow having come, and I feeling the cold very considerably, Algernon has decided to leave. Packed all our blankets, gave our tent—or what was left of it, our kettles and camping things to W——, and said good-bye to all the men. Our things were soon piled on the sledge that was to take us out of the woods, and we started.

I am glad to have had a glimpse of hunting-life in winter, also to have visited a lumber-camp. My only ideas of both have been gathered from Bret Harte; certainly his descriptions are very true and realistic, but the actual reality more hard and rough than I could have believed possible. Under such conditions men are living who might do greater things, if the wheel of fortune had arranged otherwise,—this is, of course, granting there is such a wheel!

The season for camping out with pleasure is in autumn; that time is long since past. The wintry weather and intense cold made me often glad to retreat into the shelter of our tent for fear of being frost-bitten, and all last night our rest was disturbed by the purring of a lynx close by. Algernon crept cautiously to the entrance with his rifle several times, but the night was too dark for him to get a shot. The place where we crossed the Winnipeg river ten days ago, was that same night frozen strongly enough for a waggon and team to cross the ice, and to-day our team and ourselves came over it also.

When we were leaving, after ten days spent among the lumbermen, Algernon asked what he was to pay. The foreman, who had nearly every day hunted with him, would not take any money. They all said they had "liked "so much having a visit from Mr. and Mrs. St. Maur." This from those who only knew us as strangers from a far off country which the majority had never seen, and those who had seen were never likely to see again, touched us deeply, and I realised the old truth, that some are born nature's gentlemen, and that on the other hand, how often does experience teach us that "In the midst of the "banquet of culture clowns delight to pasture on what "wise men reject as garbage."

Since leaving the woods we sent the men a supply of seventy books for winter reading; the following is a copy of the letter acknowledging them which arrived after our return to England.

To Mr. ALGERNON ST. MAUR.

DEAR SIR,—The books sent by Mrs. St. Maur came welcome to hand, and were happily received by all hands in the camp, and the boys all wish her the happiest Christmas and New Year she ever had, and they are terribly well pleased with the selection of books she made; and also I received the knife and book you sent me from New York, and I am sure I am not worthy of getting such a gift, but I will keep them in long remembrance of you and with many thanks. The snow is no deeper than when you left, and the weather much warmer.

I have one hundred and fifteen men in camp now. I wish Mrs. St. Maur was here now, she would see a difference in my camp and see how happy the men are with the books she sent them. The cook and all the men send their best respects to you both, and Karl and I our best wishes to you both, and hoping you will have a good Christmas,

I remain, yours respectfully,

WALTER WARDROPE.

CHAPTER XX.

HOMEWARD BOUND.

"What man o'er one old thought would brood and pore,
Shut like a book between its covers thin,
For every fool to leave his dog-ears in
When solitude is his, and God for evermore,
Just for the opening of a paltry door?"

On the cars en route for Ottawa, November.—Last night we were fortunate enough to secure the state room, so this morning we could dress comfortably, which is not possible elsewhere on the car.

From Winnipeg it is a three-days' journey to Ottawa, the first part mostly through "barrens" and burnt woods; the rivers which we passed were all frozen, and over everything there was a wintry mantle of thin snow and ice, while overhead the sky was grey and heavy; so that we were glad to turn away from the dreary landscape outside and amuse ourselves by reading and talking to some of our fellow-travellers.

When we entered the cars last night we were accosted by a Scotchman returning from Australia, where he had settled, and we supposed made money. He told Algernon that his heart warmed to him on seeing he was an Englishman, and he pressed him to partake of a large bottle of brandy which he produced from his pocket. Algernon declined his company and offer, which seemed to offend him, for he sat and sulked for the rest of the evening.

Two old Scotch women, a mother and daughter, were also travelling with us; they told me they had just succeeded to $40,000 by the death of the old woman's son. They would have been much better in an emigrant car, for we soon saw the old woman's only idea was to drink the whole time. Here was an instance of too much money being left to totally uneducated people doing them more harm than good.

We felt extremely sorry for a poor lady who was very ill; she was going with her husband to Montreal for advice. They had spent more than twenty years of their lives in the colonies, engaged in mission work; now she seemed quite broken down.

At Chapleau Algernon saw one of the factors of the Hudson's Bay Company, whom he had last met at Fort Alexander in 1870 when on his way to Fort Garry; he was glad to see him again and have a talk over old times.

Russell House, Ottawa, November 28th.—We were not sorry to arrive here a few days ago and settle down in comfortable rooms in this hotel.

Dined at Rideau Hall with the Governor-General and Lady Stanley of Preston; a party of twenty-six. We hear from every one, although they have but lately arrived, how much they are liked in Canada. The librarian, Monsieur de Celles, took me in to dinner, and invited us to come and see the library the following day, which we accordingly did.

Monsieur de Celles kindly took us round the library, pointing out all that was particularly interesting. There is a fine collection of 150,000 volumes, the most valuable and interesting books in the collection being those relating to the early history of Canada. Some of these were written by the Jesuit fathers as early as the 15th century; among them we saw works of De Champlain, De Salles, a history of Philip de Commines, and many others. Nearly all these books were collected in Europe, mostly in London, Paris, and Leipsic.

Champlain's surveys have been proved to be most correct; in his memoirs he mentions the loss of one of his surveying instruments; this has recently been discovered at the place indicated by him, and is now in the possession of Mr. Walter Cassels, at Toronto.

During the 17th century several Frenchmen of certain intellectual eminence from time to time made their home in Canada. Among these may be mentioned the Jesuit Charlevoix, traveller and historian; the physician Sarrasin, and the Marquis de la Galisonnière, one of the French governors of Canada.

Sarrasin, a naturalist as well as a physician, has left

his name to the botanical genus Sarracenia, of which the curious American species *S. purpurea*, the "pitcher-plant," was described by him.*

We drove to see the Chaudière Falls, a fine volume of water, for some distance a continuation of rapids extending from shore to shore; finally the mass of water rushes over an irregular wall of rock some 30 feet high. The natural beauties of the river at this place have been much destroyed by saw-mills and telegraph-lines, the poles being placed on rocks in the stream and the wires stretching across the river. Here in 1869 three men of the 60th Rifles were drowned, the small raft they were fishing from breaking from its moorings and going over the falls.

The situation of Ottawa is beautiful, and the Parliament buildings very fine; the view from the terrace round them quite magnificent. We are enjoying our little visit, the kind friends we have met here making it very pleasant.

The weather is hopeless. Much as we had wished to have some sleighing and tobogganing here, since I had never had any, it is impossible, for there is nothing but rain overhead and slush underfoot. When it does not rain it is what we call in Scotland "very saft," altogether very unusual weather in Canada at this time of year. But we read of frightful storms in the Atlantic, with blizzards at Quebec and elsewhere, so at any rate we are better off where we are.

* *Ex* Parkman's 'History of Canada.'

We visited the museum, and Professor Dawson kindly showed us many things which interested us. There is a fine collection of specimens of all the minerals, marbles, and rocks found in the Dominion. We walked through several rooms containing stuffed specimens of animals and birds. I was glad to see again my friend of the woods, the moose-bird. I found his real name was the great northern shrike, *Lanius borealis;* he has many aliases, being also called the Hudson's Bay bird.

Professor Dawson was sending specimens of seeds found this year in the mountains to the trial farms, and he most kindly gave me a small packet of the "*Castilleja pallida,*" procured on Mount Tod at an elevation of 6,000 feet. I was very anxious to obtain some roots of this plant. Unfortunately the snow was so deep when we were in the Rocky Mountains at Banff before we left that I could not find them. It grows in luxuriant clumps of fiery red, and is commonly called wild geranium from its flaming red leaves. It is got in many districts in the Rocky Mountains. Professor Dawson says it is thought that this plant possesses some of the properties of an orchid, living on the roots of other plants and trees.

Professor Dawson gave me a charming account of his explorations up the Yukon river in Alaska this summer, and showed me many photographs he had taken there. He states that most of the gold-mines on the Yukon are on British territory.

We intend to leave Ottawa to-morrow.

T

Hotel Windsor, Montreal, December 1st.—Arrived last night, and found a ball going on in the hotel. On entering the hall, a well-dressed man ran up to us and insisted on shaking us both warmly by the hand. Algernon forgets who people are, but I was much amused, remembering shortly after that it was the manager of the Dryad Hotel at Victoria. The house was horridly crowded, and, we not being ball-goers, the evening was somewhat disturbed by the sounds of music and dancing.

The *patois* spoken by the uneducated class of French Canadians is exceedingly difficult to understand, the pronunciation being so very different. Indeed, were some of this people set down in the middle of Paris, I doubt if they would be understood at all. For instance, a child comes up to us in the street and says, "*Quel tel.*" We don't understand what she wants, but a Canadian gentleman passing pulls out his watch and tells her the hour. "*Quelle heure est-il?*" was her question.

The snow has come at last, there being about six inches in the streets, and we have had two sleigh drives; the sleighs lined with buffalo robes and the drivers dressed in furs are comfortable and picturesque.

December 4th.—The weather is again wretched, so we have suddenly decided to sail on the 8th from New York. Algernon this morning met Captain Armstrong, who told him the C——s were well, and had left the Kootenay Valley, which we were glad to hear.

We are sorry to say good-bye to Canada, where we have spent so many happy months, but the prospect of home is delightful, as I am tired of wandering.

Hotel Brunswick, New York.—We arrived here yesterday; the weather beautifully bright and mild. We walked round most of the principal streets and saw the shops, and many nice carriages and well-dressed people. Here one feels instinctively that dress is more studied than in England.

The elevated railway was not quite so ugly as I expected; it looked to me like a railway bridge.

Friday.—Most hospitable are the Americans. We left one of our letters of introduction with Algernon's card before dinner last evening. In an hour or so we received a very kind note, saying that the friend to whom it was addressed would call in the morning. He duly arrived, and was most kind; promised us an excellent time if we would remain for even a week longer in New York. Alas! our plans are settled, the passages in the *Umbria* taken for to-morrow, and, after considering the matter, we think that as the weather is unusually fine and mild, we had better seize this favourable opportunity for crossing the Atlantic, as only ten days ago furious storms raged all along the Atlantic coast, causing shipwrecks and disasters of every kind.

Failing to induce us to prolong our visit, our friend

at once said, "Then we must do all we can to-day," and we start forthwith.

Firstly, he gives us a luncheon-party at Delmonico's, the well-known restaurant, where we tried the famous American dish, terrapin. Terrapin is a species of small turtle; ours was served stewed in a wine sauce, with truffles. After an excellent lunch, at which a most charming young lady made the fourth, we started for Tiffany's, the shop in New York which one ought to see. Our friend seemed well known there as a good customer, and we were shown at his request the most beautiful gems, necklaces, pearls, and other beautiful and costly things, many of them having been purchased at famous sales in Europe. This building is a great square block of five floors, and one mounts to each floor at will in an elevator, which mounts at twice the ordinary pace. We pass through endless clocks, bronzes, statuary, china, and fans, until we cry, "Enough." During Christmas week, Mr. Tiffany tells me he generally sells over $1,000,000 worth of goods.

From Tiffany's to the curio shops, from there to the tea-party of a friend our kind guide takes us. In the evening we have a pleasant dinner-party of six at his house, and this makes a charming *finale* to our few days at New York. In all countries and among all nationalities, there are interesting people and the reverse. Nowhere did we meet more pleasant men and women than in America. There is a charm and originality about the race one sees nowhere else. But there are Americans and Americans in the same way as there are pleasant people and the reverse in other countries. It is for this reason hard on the nice Americans to class them all together like a flock of sheep, often too much the way in England.

For many weeks I have been on the look-out for some pea-nuts, as one can arrange capital Chinese dolls by dressing little figures, using the nuts to form the face, hands, and feet. Now to buy pea-nuts in the street of an American town is the quintessence of vulgarity; it would be like eating hot chestnuts at a stall in Piccadilly. As we go along the street, I see a stall and a basket of pea-nuts. Algernon sighs, but we are alone and nobody knows us, so I ask the proprietor of the pea-nuts to sell me a small number; he proceeds to fill a bag, is overjoyed with the five cents I give him, and I carry off my nuts in triumph—truly the only cheap thing we have seen in New York. My triumph lasts but a short time; the paper of the bag is thin and breaks, my muff is small and won't hold them, and our friend, who is to rejoin us shortly, will be terribly shocked at my carrying such vulgar things. Happily, though, there is a large deep pocket in my gown, and into this the bag of nuts fits well, and there it remains, harmlessly enough, for the rest of the afternoon.

Saturday, December 8th.—An early start, and we are soon on board the *Umbria*. Crowds of people on the pier, seeing their friends off. A beautiful morning as we steam down the river and out into a perfectly calm sea.

Another fine day, which I enjoy whiling away the long hours watching the varied lights and shadows on the water, and a stray sail now and then.

The ship began to roll, and roll she did. Happy landsmen, who have never been to sea, write nautical songs, like "A Life on the Ocean Wave," and "Over the rolling Sea." I would advise them not to try the reality. How the ship groans! how she rocks and strains, and seems even to gasp as fresh waves strike her! I feel for the next few days too ill to live; existence is painful, and the most dismal thoughts crowd into my aching head. All our loose things fall from time to time heavily on the floor of our cabin, or roll about there. Algernon, who is an excellent sailor, sleeps peacefully the whole night. The captain and sailors call all this motion a breeze. I am thankful not to have seen a storm. I impart to the stewardess who looks after me the information that personally I would prefer the occupation of crossing-sweeper to any position of distinction on board ship. Yet she tells me that there is considerable difficulty in procuring the situation of stewardess, so many women apply for the vacant situations.

My maid was too ill to be of the slightest use to me either going or returning. They may be willing, but, as a rule, servants are not good travellers.

After six days and nine hours (then the second best passage on record), a sight of Ireland made us feel our voyage was nearly ended, and the following morning we steamed up the Mersey, and found ourselves safely at Liverpool. I felt so happy that I could have shaken hands with every one I saw.

To thoroughly enjoy home one must travel, and when far away by comparison is realized the rest, the comfort, and the repose which one finds in no other place.

LONDON:
PRINTED BY WILLIAM CLOWES AND SONS, LIMITED,
STAMFORD STREET AND CHARING CROSS.

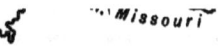

SOUTHERN PART
OF
BRITISH COLUMBIA
to illustrate
Mrs. St. Maur's travels

English Miles
0   50   100   150

Author's Route, thus:- ....

SOUTHERN PART
OF
BRITISH COLUMBIA
to illustrate
Mrs. St. Maur's travels

www.ingramcontent.com/pod-product-compliance
Lightning Source LLC
Chambersburg PA
CBHW022021240426
43667CB00042B/1037